BLACK COFFEE BLUES

BLACK COFFEE BLUES
©1992 Rollins / 2.13.61 Publications

ISBN 1-880985-05-5

THIRD PRINTING

Design: ENDLESS GRAPHICS
Back cover photo: STEVEN STICKLER

Thanx!!!: Gary I, Stan, Lynn Nakama, Mitch Bury of Adams Mass

Some kings of the road: Phil Thain, Rick Smith, Tim Pittman, Randy Ellis, Don Bajema, Hubert Selby, Dan Brewer, Black Flag.

JOE COLE: 4.10.61 - 12.19.91

2.13.61
P.O. BOX 1910 · LOS ANGELES · CALIFORNIA · 90078 · USA

2.13.61 HOTLINE #: (213)969-8043

OTHER BOOKS FROM 2.13.61:

BLACK COFFEE BLUES

124 WORLDS

#1: I got a letter from a girl today. She told me how she had come up and talked to me at a show and that I was really nice to her. She said that she was really let down. She was hoping that I would be more of a mean son of a bitch. I let her down. Next time I see her I'll kick her ass so she'll cheer up.

#2: I got three letters today telling me that I'm god. Why can't I pay the rent?

#3: He wrote me. He's doing 27 to life. He wants to know if I can send him something to read so he can pass the time.

#4: She wants to fuck me. She knows I get letters like this all the time. She knows what she wants, it's me and she wants me to hurry up and get to her town.

#5: She wants to kill herself. She wants to tell me all about it. She has been considering a few different methods and would like to know what I think of them. She likes my work and respects my opinion. She wants me to select the method I find the most fitting and she'll go for it that way. She says that it would be an honor to be dispatched by me. I told her to go die.....of old age.

#6: He doesn't get along with anyone. He doesn't fit in anywhere. I mean nowhere. Everybody hates him. Maybe everybody in the whole world. For a kid from the Midwest he sure gets around.

#7: She hates guys. She says they have their brains in their cocks. She says that she can tell that I'm different. I'm going over to her house tonight to sell her the Brooklyn Bridge.

#8: His name on the street is "Crazy B'." He's wanted on charges in connection with a homicide case in which 5 people were shot in the head execution style. He is considered armed and dangerous.

#9: He went to work. His boss got in his face because he was late. Third time this week. One more time and he would be fired. He pulled out a gun and put five shots into the bosses guts. He walked out the back door and into the sunlight.

#10: She was a junkie. She told her friends that she was going to get out of it soon. One night she went home and took too much. She died on the floor of her kitchen.

#11: She had a lot going against her. She was old. She lived alone in a high crime area. She kept a gun that her late husband had given her and taught her how to use as he was gone a lot on business. One night a man broke into her house and came into her room. She shot the man three times in the chest. She called the police. They came an hour later and took her name. They told her that she was good shot. An ambulance came and took the stiff away.

#12: He came home from work and shot himself in the head.

#13: For years she wanted to die. She never told anybody. It seemed like anything she said prompted her husband to hit her. She had three kids. One of them was retarded. One of the other children tried to fix its face by burning its cheek with a screwdriver held over the stove. Her husband rarely worked. She had to bring home the family's money. One day she was walking to work and got hit by a car.

#14: She couldn't handle her parents. Her father used to feel her up. She lost count how many times he had grabbed her breasts. As the years went by he grew more bold. It was impossible for her to have any kind of relationship with a boy. Whenever it got too far along she would see her father in the boy's face and start to cry. She couldn't tell anyone. Like anybody really wants to hear about how your father licks your throat while he rubs his fingers between your legs. Like some guy wants to hear that when he's trying to the same thing. She graduated from high school and left her parents. You should have seen her leave them. It was magnificent, stunning. Outstanding in every way. Her father couldn't believe it. She told them that she was never going to see them again. Her father yelled that she would be back. She flipped him off with her back to him as she walked down the driveway. She never came back. She moved to a big city and made a shit load of money and had a great life and never saw her parents again.

#15: He was from the Midwest. He got drafted in 1968. He was shot and killed in the jungles of Vietnam.

#16: He was a from a middle class home. He was an average student. He graduated and got an average job in the same place that his father worked. He got married to a girl that he went to school with. They had two children that looked like two children. He lived the average life of the average middle class American.

#17: She has been off heroin for three months. Everyday that goes by is a special day for her. A day that she hasn't taken drugs. Another day that she was clean, another day away from the needle. That's all she thinks about, the fact that she's no longer addicted. After work she comes home and makes herself dinner. Always the same thing, soup and a sandwich. She has to keep it together. The less she thinks the better. At the grocery store she buys two weeks worth of soup. The checkout man thinks she's crazy. She thinks it's good to be regular now that she's no longer addicted. It's not easy. Sometimes she feels bad and it's all she can do to hold on. Sometimes she sits on her bed and repeats: I don't need you, I don't need you, I don't need you.

#18: He goes to the same job every day. He comes home to his wife every night. They rarely touch each other. They're not attracted to each other any more. They don't make a big deal about it. A few years ago they would fight and swear that they were going to leave each other but then they found that when it really came down to it, neither one had the courage to go out and meet someone else. They don't hate each other. They are roommates waiting for Death.

#19: He fights a lot. He gets his ass kicked a lot. Two reasons for this: he fights when he is drunk, and he isn't all that good. He always mouths off to some large mean motherfucker who's always glad to pound the snot out of him. He does this a lot. He hates life, he hates the world. He thinks the whole place is a screaming shithole full of freaks. He sees himself as one of the only real ones out there. He reckons that they're all trying to get him and all he can do is fight, drink, take things as they come and wait for Death like a marked man waits for Death.

#20: He was raised on hate. At age six, he has quite an understanding of things. He's in fear all the time and likes to stay in his room. He doesn't smile much. There isn't anything to smile about. It's the fear and hate that he understands the best, they make sense to him and never lie. The parents lie. They lie and fight and drink and beat the shit out of everything. He figures that's the way it is. For now, the room is his friend.

#21: At age 16 he wanted to kill himself all the time. He felt alienated at his school. He would see the others and he felt nothing in common. They were so mean to him it would make your teeth ache, it would make you want to hack off one of their arms and beat the rest of them to Death with it. He thought that in Death he might find a home, perhaps find some kind of friendship. Maybe he wouldn't be so lonely and full of sadness. He was tired of the way he was feeling. Everyday was torture. One day he went home after school and shot himself in the head with his father's revolver. He left no note.

#22: She had taken all the grief that she was going to from her skinny dick piece of shit boss. All the shit that came out of that fat fuck's mouth, all that shit about how she could make a lot of money in this place if she did the right things and how lucky she was to have the job in the first place and that she shouldn't miss a chance for career advancement. Right, like she was going to go for that. What kind of woman do you think that we are dealing with here? I'll tell you what kind. She got her last paycheck, walked into his office, shot him three times and walked out. No one called the pigs and she never got caught. She cashed that check and laughs like hell every time she tells the story.

#23: He is retarded. There are things that he understands. He can get along on his own ok. The doctors say that his condition is deteriorating rapidly. Last year he understood this, now it isn't clear. He has never touched a woman. He knows that he never will. He eagerly awaits the day when he no longer feels the attraction for them. As it is right now, it hurts so much, so deeply that he cries and loses control of himself. He has caused many embarrassing moments for his family. They don't know what his problem is, why all of a sudden he'll cry and start to scream. They can't take him out anymore. He does this in public places. He's smart enough to know that he's not like the rest of them. He waits for this deep pain to end.

#24: She is a blues singer. She goes to work and sings to herself. She goes home and sings to herself. She lives alone. She sings herself to sleep at night. No one knows. No one hears her sing. At her work the other employees avoid her. She works alone on the end of the line, no one ever hears her sing. She makes up songs about everything you can imagine. She wishes she was invisible. She says: They can't see me, they can't hurt me, they don't know me, they will never touch me, they will never burn me, there's not much to life.

#25: He's from a small town. He has the same first name as his father. Two years have passed since his father took a shotgun and blew his head all over the side of the garage. No one ever found out why he did it, he seemed fine at breakfast. Now that his father is gone he lives in the house with his mother. He drives his father's car. A week after his father shot himself he opened the glove compartment looking for a map and found a receipt for the shotgun shells and a note reminding his son to take good care of the car and not to let it get too low on oil. He never showed it to his mother. She doesn't talk much anymore, she spends a lot of time sitting in the kitchen staring at the stove.

#26: School made him sick to his stomach because he had to fight all the time. He never ran away from fights. He got beat up a lot but he did win some. It seemed like every time he turned around, there was someone in his face trying to start something with him. He used to get up hours before school because his guts would be on fire getting ready to face them. One great day he punched this guy just right. A broken nose is a many splendored thing. This guy's face just exploded, it was like a rainbow, but all the colors were red.

#27: Earlier that day he got pulled out of his car and punched in the stomach by an irate cab driver he had accidentally cut off in traffic. The incident upset him so much that he had to go to the executive washroom and vomit. Now he looks at himself in the mirror. He always thought that he looked rather bad in that kind of light. His face always looked bluish like he was dead. He looks at his face and all he can think is that he's a coward. He hates himself.

#28: PCP#1: They have strange pets in this neighborhood. Part cat, part lizard, part snake, part rat. They coil and snap on the front porches, some of them go to work. They kill lost children. They skin them and hang them like trophies in the wall, they bury the bones in the backyard. There might be some in mine. I'll go check when I get the guts to walk out there. So far I can't face it. Last time I went out, one of the animals came at me teeth first. Shining like a stolen moment under the crime lights. If I wanted to I could kill all the fuckers with my thoughts, no really I could. I could bad trip them, make them slaughter themselves during commercial breaks when they get up to feed. At some point I will kill you. You know that already.

#29: We walk down the street debating, should we take a cab, bus, or should we walk to the graveyard. I say that I don't mind walking. She says she doesn't think I'm up to it and hails a cab.

We get to the graveyard and walk thru the gate. I feel hesitant. Not because I have a problem with walking past a bunch of stiffs, but because I think that some kind of custodian or cop is going to come out of the little shack at the front and give us shit about what the hell we were planning on doing in the graveyard. I could see it plain as day, some fat piece of shit pig: "What do you think you're going to do in here? You're looking for a place to screw aren't you? Yea, I figured as much, you little sluts...you think you're going to go into one of those mausoleums and screw your little goddamn brains out don't you, well you're not. You get the hell out of here before I kick your shit all the way down to the station...I see you looking at me fella, go on try something, I want you to, I'll hit you so hard your mamma will get a black eye, get the hell out of here you little shits..." Something like that. We go past the gates, no one comes out. We walk down the uneven, cracked pathway.

Whole families lined up in rows. Some stones just say "BABY." Small stones with numbers are all over. These are plots for sale. I think of a man walking down the path with the caretaker after they have had a cup of coffee and a few laughs. The man looks down at a stone and says to the caretaker "Here. This is the place, is this taken? I want my body put right here. Still open? Great, how much, oh great. Yes I like the way the sun catches it, not near any trees, good, I don't want birds getting anything on my stone, not that I'll know anything about it. Yes that's a joke, yes I believe that you've heard it all before, but yes, I'll take it."

If I were going to pick a place where my body was going to rest for eternity, I would want to be really sure of the place, I mean really sure. I would set up a tent and camp out at the spot for a few days. I know that it would look a bit strange, like if there was a funeral nearby and all these mourners file past my bright orange tent. I'd smile and wave as I tended to my franks and beans cooking on the sterno stove. I would stick out without question, but at the end I would know for sure. I would walk up to that caretaker and with a steady eye and a voice that defined conviction, I'd say "Yes sir, that's the grave for me, you betcha. Where do I sign." I would mean it and he would know it.

I suggest that this place would be a great golf course, it has a pond and everything. It would take a mighty golfer to be able to get thru the course what with all the stones in the way, a real challenge. I mean come on, pro golfers must get bored of these tournaments. These big ass fields, every once in awhile an alligator or something. Imagine the fun these guys would have playing thru a mausoleum. What if a golfers ball landed on his long lost uncle's grave. Ok, my dad used to walk his dogs on this golf course on the weekends. The course was huge. The dogs ran around and had a great time. The dogs were faithful and good, they would see those balls flying thru the air and they would retrieve them and place them like a little pile of quail eggs at my father's feet. From hundreds of yards away I could see golfers shaking their fists. Although the distance was great, I could still hear what they were saying. A lot of shit about "Godammit, shit, dogs...my ball!" My dad would laugh his ass off. Sometimes he was almost human.

We walk over to a mausoleum all decked out in iron and granite. The room inside is bigger than a lot of apartments I've lived in. She thinks that there might be passages underneath it. I ask her what she thinks a bunch of dead guys are going to do with secret passage ways. I can see them all down there laughing, "Haw, haw, our wives still think we're dead, hey Moe, pass that over here, haw haw...." You never know, so I go over and put my ear to the door and listen for the blare of a stereo, the crash of bowling pins....nothing, not a sound.

We keep walking. I trip over a wreath and knock it over. I pick it up and put it back on its stand. I read the name on the stone "Sorry John, I mean Mr. Garland." I walk away and look back, the wreath has fallen over again. I know that if there really is a hell, I'm going to be there and old John Garland will be pissing on my head from a cloud on high.

We have walked all the way around and we're close to the gate again. I look over and I see what looks like a television antenna poking out from behind a stone. I walk over there and check it out, it's just a wreath stand turned over. It would be great to see a pair of rabbit ears clipped onto a stone, a repair guy out there hooking the grave up for cable. Hey we got big screen TV, grab a shovel and come on in.

There's every type of stone you can think of in here. I point out one that looks like a big ebony dick. She looks at me and starts laughing. I suggest that some of these people should have gotten their loved ones to put some fancy custom neon work on their stones, that would really stand out amongst all the gray and black.

We get to the gate, I hear some voices. I look over and see three guys in workman uniforms leaning up against a truck passing a joint between them. I tell her that David Lee Roth's grave will have a full bar and a merchandising booth. We leave the graveyard.

#30: He had the day off. He sat in the room. That's what he did when he wasn't at the job. The job made him hate. Made him hate endlessly. Made him punch the wall. Made him keep his fucking mouth shut. It felt good to grind his teeth. He would walk home from the shift hoping that someone would fuck with him so he could use his fists.

It was the day before christmas. Like many christmasses past he didn't send nor receive presents or cards. To him christmas was another day. Just another day to be followed by another one. He knew they were full of shit because they needed a special day of the year to be nice to each other. They couldn't just be that way, they needed an occasion to come out of their holes and be human beings. What rotten shits they were. He knew this. It always boiled down to money for them. There was no escape. Life was just waiting for the next shift to start.

He remembered the christmasses of his youth. He was living

with his mother. She would get him some presents and never let him forget for a minute that he was a pain in her ass. She would pull out the plastic christmas tree from the closet and put it up with the same lights from the year before, it was a sad ritual. He remembered how she always had a cigarette hanging out of her mouth and would tell him that he had better appreciate this shit. She put "Goddamn" before everything she said. Goddamn presents, goddamn toys, etc. He wanted to tell her that he didn't care about the tree and the presents and could she not be so nasty all the time. She was scaring him and he hadn't done a thing to deserve it. He didn't make up christmas. Opening the presents was a drag. He knew that she really couldn't afford the presents and buying them made her angrier than usual. She would say "You better enjoy that one, I paid a lot of goddamn money for that." She would light up a cigarette and watch him like a hawk. He did his best to look happy when he opened the presents. In truth he had no interest in them. All he wanted to do was kill her. He could tell by the things that she got for him that she didn't know anything about him. It was like having a crazy woman paying your rent and buying you shit and telling you that she wished you didn't exist.

At christmas time, his mother's mother would call. Grandmother was a drunk. He met her a few times and she was always fucked up, slurring her words, make up on all crooked, falling over chairs, laughing. They would get on the phone and his mother would start screaming, her cigarette ashes falling all over the floor. Finally his mother would slam the phone down and start breaking things in the kitchen. He would run to his room and hide.

A few days later he would be sent over to his father's house to visit and collect presents that had been bought for him. Sometimes there was a christmas tree but most times there wasn't and that was big relief. His presents were always in the closet next to his father's boots. The presents were never wrapped, he could tell that his father didn't know him at all. His mother would give him a box of cigars to take over to his father for a present. Father would look at them and put them on a shelf and say nothing. His father would watch a football game on TV and fall asleep in his easy chair with a lit cigar in his hand. He would watch his father sleep, debating if he should let the cigar burn his father's hand. At the last minute he would gently remove the cigar and put it in the ashtray.

Later on there was the overcooked dinner served up by his stepmother. She was a terrifying and unpleasant bitch, common. She would never use sugar, she put artificial sweetener in everything. The meal was dry and neglected. A hateful heap of shitty food. He would get a sharp poke in the ribs from his father signifying that it was time for him to say something nice about the meal. "Real good ma'am." His father would look at him and nod. She made it clear that he was a pain in her ass. He couldn't wait to leave, she scared the shit out of him.

He would go back to his mother's house with all the presents from father. His mother would pull it all out and look it over, muttering as she went thru the lot. "Goddamn, he really is a goddamn slob isn't he. How do you work this goddamn thing.." She would force a moving part on of one of the toys, breaking it. "See, this goddamn stuff is cheap. You see what a cheap bastard he is, christ."

He would pull the presents into his room and put them in a pile in the corner. He rarely played with the things that they bought him. He was scared to break them. She would hit him, call him ungrateful and threaten to have the police come and take him to jail forever. "I'm thinking about calling the police and having them take you away. How would you like that?" Whack. "How...whack...would...whack...you...whack...like...whack...that?"

He sat and thought out loud. "I should have let you burn your whole fucking house down dad, just what you needed." Another christmas going by. He sat and watched the snow fall by the window, nice view from where he was, another apartment building. He could see a few christmas tree lights blinking, the occasional head pass by. The heater was making small rattling sounds like it was shivering. "Yea you and me both pal ha ha."

Tomorrow another day off, another day to wait until the shift started again. The shift would always start again. Any time away from the job was just spaces in its big teeth, little gaps in which you were allowed to breathe and lie to yourself and make yourself think that you were alive. They had you coming and going. They had you, there was nothing but the shift and the apartment. The work and the wait. He spent his off time resting, soaking his feet in hot water to keep the swelling down, it was endless. The room was poorly lit. There were three sockets in the ceiling but he never replaced the bulbs after they burned out. He was now down to one. Darkness came, the snow kept falling. He sat and waited for the shift to start.

#31: He said that he was free. He told us that no one was as free as he was. We shook our heads and made humorous asides as we waited for the official papers to be handed to the secretary so we could read the Death sentence right to his face. Let him tell us all about his freedom. When he heard the verdict he didn't even flinch, in fact, and you can check me on this, his eyes opened wide and a great smile broke across his face. "Such is total freedom" he said and closed his eyes.

#32: It was her third black eye in one year. She didn't freak out. She did shoot him in the back of the head while he was watching television.

#33: The doctor asked her why she would look out the window

and never look at him when she spoke. She turned and looked at him. "In my garden I am free, you can't touch me, the trees are blue and gold, it's all blue and gold, it doesn't matter where you put me, I will always see the colors. You will die because you're obsessed with Death, you reek of Death, this office, Death. You have Death in your eyes, you have a Death ray coming out of your forehead. It must be angry that I can see it. I used to be one of you, that's how I know your disease. You will kill almost everything, of course you won't kill me because I know how to deal with human garbage like you." She turned and looked out the window.

#34: He watched a lot of television. He didn't care what was on, he was picking up information. It was all re-con. Every hour that he watched, the more he knew about them, about how they worked, their patterns. The more he knew, the easier it was going to be to take action when the time came. He was on a mission of classified status. Protocol demanded that all details of the operation be kept out of general circulation. This was after all, a matter of national security. At work all his fellow employees knew that he was crazy. He knew that his cover was intact. It wasn't everyday a top agent used a packing company as a cover. This was fine with him. He used this to work without raising his profile, easier to get into their lives and see how they ticked. The more information the better.

Back at the house he watched the television nonstop. He took notes furiously, the woman in the shampoo ad would scratch her ear the same way every time she did the ad, in fact her movements and speech patterns were so precise that he could swear it was the same ad every time. He made a note to get all possible information on life-like robots. That was another thing he knew about her, about them all. From his in-depth notes: "They lack any kind of style, definitely a cult of personality, it's easy to see that they are used to lying and getting lied to, in fact from my estimation, they use lies as their primary means to exchange information. When dealing with them, use lies to befriend them. Employ the truth to confuse and debilitate them...must get more information."

Years went by. There was a security leak. Actually it was Norm who saw a notebook on Larry's desk that had "Classified Stuff-Top Secret Mission-No peeking!!!" People at work would ask "How's the mission going Larry?" He would tell them that he knew of no mission, that even if he did have knowledge of any so-called mission that he wouldn't be at liberty to disclose the details of such a mission, even if it did exist. The piles of notebooks grew higher. He found a new and fantastic place to pick up information, the library. They were always whispering in there. They must be exchanging secret lies. He would go into the library and pretend to look thru the books. He even went as far as to get himself a library card. Every once in awhile he would take out books to make them think that he was a fan of literature. He usually selected books that he had already read (Old Man and the Sea, White Fang, One Flew Over the Cuckoo's Nest, etc.) so he would be able to answer questions in case the librarian attempted to spot-quiz him. Keeping all the bases covered is a principle detail in top security work, you have to be at your sharpest and best at all times.

#35: The guy turned on his barstool and faced him. He told him that in no uncertain terms he could kick his ass one-handed. The two of them went outside. The man who made the boast took out a handgun and shot the other man in the chest twice, one-handed.

#36: They were on the couch watching television. He had his arm draped over her shoulder. They watched a program about a group of young lawyers full of compassion and human values battle for the rights of society's underprivileged. A young man had been accused of raping a woman. He was in court now, trying to plead his case. The girl on the couch said "He's guilty." He asked her how she knew, thinking that perhaps she had already seen this episode. "I know he did it, a woman can always tell. We know how men are, yes he definitely did it." He looked at her "What a load, I know how women are. They say that they want it but if they don't like it or they get pregnant or something, they yell rape, and the guy goes to jail, it's a pile of shit I think. If they didn't want men coming up and trying to get next to them then why do they wear the clothes that they do. It's a mean fucked up game if you ask me, women have men by the balls and sometimes the weaker of them loses control after getting their dicks teased thru the roof." She looked back at him like he had just dumped a bucket of llama shit on her head and asked for a dollar. "You think it's ok for some guy to do what he wants to a woman, that the clothes she wears are an invitation for gratuitous sex? If that's your attitude, I'm leaving right now, men are pigs!" "No!" he shot back. "That's not what I meant at all, I don't think some guy can do what he wants to a woman, come on what do I look like...damn." "Ok" she said "I know what you mean about the teasing thing, I hate to say this, but me and my friends used to do it when we were younger and not as classy as we are now, ha ha. We used to get guys all hot and bothered and see how far we could go before it got too heavy and then we would leave. Just leave, like bye bye, you know. It was fun for awhile but I can see how it would drive a man wild." He reached down and cupped her breast, she looked at him and smiled. He kissed her and worked his hand into her shirt, he got his hand into her bra and outlined her nipple with his finger, with his other hand he went up her skirt. He had his hand in her panties now and was running it thru her pubic hair. She slowly removed his hand from her shirt and held it, she took his index finger into her mouth and ran her tongue around its tip and looked into his eyes. She took her other hand and placed it on the bulge in his pants. A commercial came on. An ad for milk. A beautiful girl drank a glass of milk, licked her lips and said "Ummm, yummy." The beautiful girl smiled and the ad went off. She squeezed the bulge and said "Ummm, yummy." She started unbuttoning his shirt, kissing the places where the buttons had been, she dug her tongue into his navel as she undid his belt. She pulled his cock out and started talking to it. "Hello handsome, you look so good I could eat you like candy. I bet you taste so good. You're so big and strong, what's a poor girl to do? I can't control myself!" He could feel her breath on his cock. She looked up at him and smiled. He closed his eyes and let out a long sigh, this was going to be great. She gave his cock a slight tug and laughed as she got up. "That's the kind of stuff that we used to do, god weren't we mean! Those poor guys must have hated our guts! Well look, I've got to go, me and the girls are going to go down and see that new Ted Bundy documentary. Have you ever seen him, he is so hot. All my friends want to rip his clothes off. If any of them call here looking for me, tell them I am on my way, bye!"

#37: It was a Thursday night. He went into the 7-11 to get some coffee. He got his cup and put a cream in it. He stood behind this Filipino looking guy who was pouring himself a cup. He checked the guy out, he had an earring. What a fag he thought to himself. The guy moved so he could get to the coffee. He was reaching for the pot, but the guy stopped again to get one of those stirrer things. The nerve of this guy he thought to himself, like he had all the time in the world. "Hey come on let's go" he said to the guy. The guy turned around and stared right thru him like he wasn't there and slowly moved to the cash register. Our boy reached for the pot found it was empty. The Filipino guy turned around and gave him a winning smile as he walked out the door. He didn't feel like waiting for the next pot to be made and he was mad too, so he decided to leave. He walked past a VW and saw a cup of coffee sitting on its roof. He figured it must be that asshole's car. Someone tapped him on the shoulder. He turned and got punched squarely in the mouth. It was the Filipino, his friend was there too. Before he knew what was going on, he was hit again. He tried to hit back and was leveled by a kick to the head. The guy's friend was roaring with laughter "How you like that John Wayne?" he said as he laughed his ass off. Our boy got up and was met by another fist to the face. He felt teeth break. He thought to himself: I'm getting my ass kicked in the parking lot of a 7-11 for nothing, for bullshit, oh christ. The Filipino looking guy merrily punched the shit out of our boy until he vomited and passed out in the parking lot. Another night.

#38: He wasn't stupid, he didn't get off the truck yesterday. He saw all things, perhaps more clearly than you might think. He used to do the angry young man thing when he was younger but he was no longer young and he felt no need to play that shit. He went up to the roof of his apartment and threw himself off. Like I said, he wasn't born yesterday. He knew full well that he was not a bird, he knew that he would fall like a stone and splatter on the ground.

#39: I walk the straight lines. I walk thru the summer nights. I walk the silver rope of dreams. I walk thru dawns of dawns. There's not a lot that isn't dying. I see people parading in front of each other like insects in a killing jar watching each other die. I walk the straight lines thru the christ machines, thru the eyes of the throw away people, thru the wards and the shores and the cracks in the skulls of the sidewalks, thru love's howling vacancy. I am the freedom soil, I dig my own grave, I resurrect myself every night. I am all things to myself. I walk the straight lines, I walk the spider's jail house. I walk the think line, the thin line, the white line and all the lines in between. I wish I could trade in my eyes.

#40: It was near two in the morning. The old man was crossing Sunset Blvd. His name was Cedric and he drank wine. Earlier that evening he had offered to park a car for a yuppie couple on their way into a restaurant. The yuppie male wanted to punch good old Cedric's lights out for even talking to him. The yuppie female cooled him out, the male gave Cedric a five dollar bill to show her how in control of his macho shithead emotions he was. He would use this as a bargaining ploy to get up her skirt later on that night. She knew it and thought that it was a cute gesture. Just so you know, it worked. Anyway, good old Cedric was crossing the street and a car turning left crossed in front of him. Cedric noticed that the car's lights were off and he yelled at the driver to turn his lights on, he could cause an accident. Cedric was very observant about things like this. At that moment a young boy popped up in the back seat, he couldn't have been more than 15 years old. The boy fired two .22 slugs into Cedric's stomach. Cedric folded onto the intersection of Sunset and Maltman. The car drove off. Just be glad it wasn't you. Now shut the fuck up and watch some MTV.

#41: He was my hero so I watched him closely. Yea, he said all the things that I wished I had said, the things I wished I had the guts to say. You know it was all the truth but damn, I couldn't just come out and say it like he did. He was driven by hate, absolutely fueled by hatred. I liked to hear them try to turn him around. They would come on with all this soft sell crap. He would flatten them with his resolve. Their rose colored glasses cracked right into their eyes. They would try to run guilt trips on him, telling him what his problem was. What did they know, they never even left their houses. I would never say a word one way or the other. I just watched and listened. It was great to see all their bullshit fall on the ground in front of him, he wasn't going to go their way. I didn't always agree with him. Some of the things he said were too extreme for me, but I liked knowing that he was around. Yea, he made no bones about how he felt. It's not the kind of language I like to use, but the best way to put it was; he didn't give a fuck about what they thought and what they thought about him. I wish I could say that, I still think of him.

#42: They were parked in the lot in front of the Frontier Market. It was Friday night and this was the second time they had gone out. The first time was a few nights ago and she had reckoned that he was an ok guy and that was it. She hadn't thought about him at all until he had called her again tonight and asked her if she wanted to "go hang out." She had said yes. So there they were parked in the lot and she was getting ready to give him the rap to cool him out because she didn't want to get into a heavy thing with this guy. She wasn't about to get into it with anyone in a parking lot. They sat there. Finally she asked him what the fuck they were doing. He told her that they were "hanging out." From the outside it looked like they were waiting for something. Looking straight out the window without expression. Hell maybe they were waiting for Death. That shit happens, people get it into their heads that it's time to check out and they buddy up and do it together in a car. Happens at shopping malls all the time. You think I'm kidding you, slap your mother if you think I'm kidding. Right. She gets all uptight because it occurs to her that her time is getting wasted here. She tells him to take her home, she doesn't have time for this shit. The guy starts to freak out, tells her that he really wants to talk to her. She says alright what do you want to talk about. He looks out the window, he doesn't know, he just wants to talk, to make contact. When was the last time you wanted to say it all to the right person. To have it all come out right, to surprise yourself at how together you could be. When was the last time you ever met someone that made you want to give it all to them, I mean give yourself to them, where you couldn't express yourself enough, like you wanted to cut off one of your arms to be understood. That's it, you would cut your head off to have someone understand you, and you know how pointless that one is. You know how many times you've smashed yourself to bits on the rocks. Did you hear about the man that met the wonderful girl? She kissed him and he felt alive again. Yea, he was burned out on women, burned out on any kind of dealings with humans, they made him sick. He had become so cynical over the last few years that he had it in his mind that he would never meet anyone who could ever matter to him. Do you know what happened to that guy? He met this girl and she made him see that he was wrong. After he spent a short time with her he felt all those old feelings come back. She brought him back to life. But anyway, these two in the parking lot. The guy is sweating now because he wants to tell her everything, whatever that is. A man walks over to the car and asks "Do one of you have a light?" They both reply no. The man takes out a pistol and shoots them in the face and legs. He runs out of the parking lot right onto Hollywood Blvd and disappears. Have you ever been in love? I mean real love, love where you forget everything and make an ass out of yourself and not care? Do you have an idea of what the inside of that car looked like after that guy ripped up those two? A lot of blood, a lot of hair on the back seat. California sucks. Someone should just drop a bomb on the place and give it back to the roaches. Before I fuck your mother, I'm going to break her arm.

#43: He sat at the end of the bar alone and listened to the traffic outside. What a bunch of animals out there, shit. You have to get loaded to get up the guts to make the walk home, the way these people act these days. How many drinks had he already had? On a night like this he didn't count. The guy behind the bar had the radio turned to some shitty station where all the music sounded like you were days away from dying, you know that dead ass music that comes on, you can't believe anyone could make music like that let alone listen to it. His mind wandered as it always did, to all the things that he had tried to do over the years and had fucked up. He had great capacity for regret and self pity. He thought he was alone. He had no idea that he was like a lot of people. He had been told before that he was pathetic for the way he dragged himself around sometimes. Women would give him a lot of shit, telling him to just get up and "be a man." When he heard things like that, he would straighten up for a time. Some woman telling him to be a man. Right, like a woman could know anything about being a man. What a crock of shit. Someone should have told him that everybody does the self-pity-wallow-down-in-the-dumps-hard-swallow-routine. People are always so fast to give someone else shit for the things that they do themselves, for the things that they themselves are. Aided the booze, his thoughts became sullen and hard. There was no life, there was no real happiness. His apartment stank and he lived alone. In the morning he would go to work and take shit from a guy that was 7 years younger than he was. Something hit him hard. He had fallen off his stool and was on the floor. He got up. The bartender looked at him and asked him if he was alright. He nodded, paid and left. He got back to the room and sat on the edge of the bed for a long time. Finally he walked over to the toilet and vomited. He could get it all in without making a mess. After a decade of puking you get good at it, your throat relaxes and you can let go with no problem. One of the benefits of being a drunk fuck-up. If he had a gun he would have shot himself that night. For him it was all a joke. He didn't waste time losing sleep thinking about women. At his age, with the way he looked he wouldn't get fucked unless he was paying and that idea was too pathetic for him to think about. Years ago he would have cried and turned on the radio and stared at the ceiling. He was past that kind of thing now. The city had filled his veins with stale nights of truth and dried blood. Have you ever seen a dried pool of blood after the ambulance has taken the body away? Like outside a liquor store, with the neon reflecting off of it? Some poet could write some up-the-ass thing about that pool of blood. If it hasn't been hosed off, it's wild to walk by it the next day and look at it in the daylight, it's more intense than looking at a wine cooler ad. The city had turned life into a process, a ritual where he knew he was poisoning himself and he couldn't care less. He could see how stupid it was to even try. People were cheap, all the shit that came out of their mouths. Fucking murderers, animals, dirt breathers. Goddamn, this is such a lonely place. Don't ask me my name, just stay here with me. I think if I'm alone tonight I will die in my sleep.

#44: His struggle was long and well documented. A lot of people passed thru his life. There were long stretches of brightness, times when I thought he wasn't human. The way he could keep going when it made me tired just to watch. His grip at times was unbelievable. His rise was a lesson to all. A slap to the face of any that ever doubted him. His ascension was like an iron fist punching thru the sky. His driving force was rage. When he achieved anything, he would think to himself that he had beaten them again. He had proven himself to them all. When he was low on inspiration, he would think of them and his desire to utterly destroy them. A surge of energy that he could barely contain would shoot thru him. At times he felt absolutely electric, incredibly strong. There was a dangerous and negative aftereffect to all this. He suffered periods of depression that made it hard to breathe. At times, he thought that he would kill himself. For years he had tried to relate to women, he was always unsuccessful.

No matter who he met, after a short time he felt distant and alienated. They never understood his need to confront, his need to challenge. When he would tell them that he wanted to die all the time, that there was beauty in pain, they never understood. In his mind there was only truth. He ignored any suggestion that was ever offered him. He prided himself in being able to take the punishment year after year. The secret was this: he had no fear of Death. He was truly ready to die at all times. He hated life. He had pure contempt for it. His conduct bordered on violent paranoia. No one understood what he was after. You should have heard all the bullshit that dropped out of their mouths when they talked about him, like they could ever last a minute in his shoes, like they ever could experience the pain thresholds that he had. He knew things they never would. They never pushed themselves to any heights, they never aspired to anything except being spectators and judges. They were cowards. He would look into their eyes and they knew that he knew. I watched and learned from him. I knew what he was trying to do, all I can say is that he pulled it off. Right in your fucking face. That's why I can't look at any of you little bimbos and freaks seriously. You have no character, no guts. Nothing.

#45: He wanted to talk to people about god. He would stop them on the street. Sometimes he would just sit alone and talk out loud about his great love for god and all the joy that he was bringing to the world with his word. He was filled with love for people even though they never listened to him, or even worse told him to fuck off, took swings at his head. "Get the fuck out of here you dick!" This guy wearing a Black Sabbath Vol 4 shirt and flashing a large knife chased him for two blocks screaming "For Ozzy, for Satan, for Van Gogh!" over and over. Life was hard for this jesus loving piece of shit. A few weeks ago some kids set him on fire while he was sleeping in the park.

#46: He was from one of the many shitholes in the beach cities of Southern California. He was a moron, if you saw where he came from, you would understand why he resembled a garden salad with legs and a cigarette. These towns, shit. They all look like they were built in the mid 70's in 20 minutes time. All over, abandoned shopping malls. Mile after mile of flat relentless nothing. There was one apartment building where a man hacked up a woman and put her in garbage bags. He was called the Glad Bag Killer. That was a long time ago and it's only an apartment building, it's not like they still have the glad bags there so you can see inside. So yea, if you grew up in a place like this, sniffing liquid paper would seem like a great way to spend an afternoon. He used to work at a gas station on Aviation Blvd. He would eat at a Winchell's Donuts across the street because he liked the chili. He was gone two days when his body was discovered under the Redondo Beach pier. The pigs said that he died from a blow to the head.

#47: He worked. He worked and worked and worked. He drank. He drank and drank and drank. He walked home from work the same route every day. He checked all the pay phones for change, he pressed all the crosswalk buttons. One night he got home and found that he had forgotten his wife's name.

#48: She was the woman with no name. She came in when they were leaving their offices to go home for the day. Some of the staff tried to be polite and said hello in passing. She never said a word back, she just looked at the ground and nodded slightly. She was there to clean and that's all. She knew the truth. The truth was that none of these people would give her the time of day if she was outside the building. None of these people would ever be caught dead in her neighborhood and they all made more money in two days than she made in a week. She liked it best when they were all gone. She liked the cool clean quiet of the offices. Nothing like the howling sty she lived in. The smell of fried food and the non-stop arguing of the families on either side of the apartment that she shared with with her family: her husband's sister's family and her own mother. The offices smelled like power and security. Sometimes she sat behind a desk and looked out the window at the lights of the city. She didn't want to go home.

#49: He came home from school to find his mother on her hands and knees in front of the television set. She had been drinking wine and had spilled a large glass on the rug. She was trying to clean it up, but she was drunk as shit and she wasn't making much headway. She looked like a cow, she was pathetic. Whenever she drank things fell over. That was the usual. He would be in his room and would hear the dull thud of her falling over, or the shrill sound of glass breaking. He never got used to it either. He would jump like some shell shocked motherfucker every time he heard her destroy something. (For years afterwards he would jump at small sounds in his apartment, glass breaking in restaurants made his skin crawl.) Today's horrifying raft of shit was another slurred speech about what a fucker his father was. He barely remembered seeing them together. He went to see his father from time to time, he couldn't understand how they got together in the first place. He couldn't think of two more different people. You know that "opposites attract" bullshit? These two weren't even opposites, they were from different tribes, different planets. Get it straight, both of them were fucked in their own way, totally fucked. He hated them both and knew that he was going to go a lot farther than they ever did because they were pieces of shit and he was awesome. She was equipped with a non-stop mouth. One of hell's many gates was planted squarely in the middle of her face. He stopped listening to her a long time ago. He helped her clean the red wine out of the carpet as best he could and went to his room. He locked the door against any sneak attack that she might try. She would do that, bum rush his room to yell at him about some shit like she had a clue to anything smacking of reality. She would try the "I'm your mother!" line to beat on him with her little bird fists. He could have put his fist clean thru her head, but he was so far past that stage it wasn't even funny. He put his headphones on and for a little while, he was out of there.

#50: She was on her way home from a friend's house. A man raped her in the parking lot of her apartment building, 30 feet from the entrance. At first she begged him to let her go. He punched her, broke the left half of her jaw. She stopped resisting, it was better to just get it over with and hope that he didn't kill her. All the time he was raping her she could feel it, she didn't black out. She could feel him tearing her up inside. She tried to relax so it would hurt less. Her jaw made bright blue sparks flash in front of her eyes every time he pushed in. Suddenly it was over. He ran away. She stumbled inside, someone on the first floor watched it happen but didn't think it was anything serious, just kids fooling around. Her roomate saw her when she came in and called the police and soon an ambulance came. This was three years ago. Since then she's had recurring nightmares. She has lost more than half a dozen jobs. Her bosses say she lacks motivation. She is on heavy dosages of anti-depressants. She can no longer carry on a normal relationship with a man. The last one that touched her was the one that raped her. He was the second man she had ever had sexual contact with. When her father came to visit her and put his arms around her, she nearly vomited on his shoes.

#51: He got off work and went to a bar. He drank until he was drunk. He went outside and turned his hand into a fist and hit a brick wall and broke three knuckles. He vomited and passed out. He woke up and started weaving his way home on foot. He didn't feel the pain from his hand. When he got to his place, he found that he had lost his keys. He kicked the door down and passed out on his couch. Another night that reeks of blood and gin, frustration and an overwhelming all consuming sense of loss.

#52: What a joke, life, big deal. He put the gun to his head and put it down. He put it under his chin and put it down. He watched a little television. He talked some small talk on the phone, hung up. He put the gun in his mouth. Little thoughts, little dreams. He put the gun down. He laughed, he knew he was full of shit.

#53: He worked at a steel cutting place in El Segundo. He went in at 6 pm and came out around 3 am. Like a lot of his friends that worked there, he drank on his way to work as well as on shift. His usually started with two Bud tall boys that he drank out of paper bags in the back of the bus. Sometimes he would see some of his friends on the bus. They would raise their bags in salute and say in unison "I love my job!" Drinking was a way to get thru the boredom of the job. It was a dangerous thing to do, almost every employee had a near accident, nearly losing a finger or a hand to one of the machines. Signs were all over the facility warning that even the slightest lapse of caution could lead to severe mutilation. The men would joke and say that there was a delicate balance to be struck. You had to be sober enough to do your work and not get fired or mutilated but be drunk enough to where when you did fuck up, you wouldn't feel it. One night he went in a bit more drunk than usual. He lost his right hand two inches past his wrist. The amount of blood that came from the arm was unbelievable. He didn't feel a thing.

#54: He shot that dude like it was nothing, I never seen anything like it in my life. He pulled up to the red light, got out of his car. He walked over to the Plymouth and fired three shots into the driver's face. He then got back into his car. He had the music up loud, some heavy metal garbage. I've never seen anything like it! He just wasted the fucker! Anyway, the light turned green and he took off, and so did everybody else except for the dead guy.

#55: Ever since he got back, he's had trouble sleeping. It seems like every time he closes his eyes he sees a bright light shining thru his lids like oncoming headlights. The nightmares never stop coming. Every day is filled with grey ghosts and dead bodies behind the couch, a burnt arm on top of the television set. The backyard is a mine field, you could get your balls blown off out there. Electrified fence in his mind. Never let the fuckers under the wire. If they get in under the wire, they'll kill you and keep killing you, hack and keep hacking. Villages never stop burning.

#56: PCP 2: I wear my sunglasses. Keeps you on one side and me on the other. I don't know you, you'll never know me. What's the word? Thunderbird! I keep the devils to the side. I keep the good on the inside and the bad on the outside. All you see is the bad, got me? What's your bag? Do you dip into the goody bag or the devil bag? What's your truth, where did it go, what happened? You got to wear your sunglasses and keep your radio tuned to Black Sabbath!

#57: He wanted to get real. All he saw was a bunch of fakes. He hated them all. They needed to get a lesson in what the real thing was, this was the thing that he was going to show them, and show them good. Shove them right down their own throats. He was going to show them all by shooting every pig on the force. He didn't do it, he shot two pigs that were parked in a 7-11 parking lot. They were kissing. Both head shots. Good placement, an outstanding job. Their boyfriends back home would barely be able to recognize them at the morgue. He was off to an amazing start. He had potential, but he quit. Hey man, don't ever quit. Don't ever give up your dreams, go on and on till the break of dawn. Thanx!!

#58: Two angels were kicking back on a park bench in one of god's green pastures, Angel #1 pulls out a cigarette coated with PCP.

Angel #1: Hey homey check this shit out.

Angel #2: Where the fuck did you get that?

Angel #1: I got some friends down in LA.

Angel #2: Lets torch that bad boy!

Angel #1: Serious smoke!

The two angels smoked the dummy and got down right stupid.

Angel #1: I'm fucked up!

Angel #2: Lets take him out.

Angel #1: Who?

Angel #2: The big guy, lets cap his ass, fuck it.

Angel #1: Go ballistic on the punk just like that?

Angel #2: You know it.

Angel #1: What's the matter, don't you like it here?

Angel #2: I don't know about you but it's been too long since we fucked some shit up. Lets go get some like we used to do.

Angel #1: You're right, we should have rolled this from the git go!

The two angels pulled up in front of god's crib and cold smoked his ass in a flurry of buckshot.

#59: Iron Man turned to steel in the great magnetic field. Fuck you. Iron Man goes out at night and shoots people in the face at close range and never gets caught. He kills pigs and walks away. This fucking freak show, bimbos, transvestites, faggot nightmares, assorted human garbage. Now that he is here to strike fear, your bullshit falls thru the cracks. All your liberal coward humanitarian lies crawl away to die. You garbage eaters. Useless hustlers. Trash falling out of your mouth. Who the fuck are you going to call to help you? You have no one to call, can't you see that you should have been swept off the streets and burned with the rest of the waste years ago? Can't you see that you were just a walking mistake, an oversight. He didn't mean to let this go so far. I guess he figured you were going to do the right thing and shoot yourself in the face a long time ago. That's why he shoots you in the face, so others can see how ugly you really are. Nice work, he just shoots people for what you would think is "no reason." That's because you're so fucked up. You think that life owes you. When you and 11 other disease bags are shot in the face at close range on a public bus, you see the truth. Life doesn't owe you shit. If there was a god he wouldn't let a guy walk right up and shoot you in the face now would he? That's right, now you get the picture. Truth burns doesn't it? Look at the statistics. He kills and keeps killing. He keeps winning. You can't escape the truth. This is Darwinism on speed. This had to happen. Soon all will be loneliness. Panic. You will see yourself.

#60: If you called him a coward he would come back at you with a recount of his participation in some epic act of violence. If you called him a typical macho shithead, he would grin and start laughing. He said that there wasn't a woman on earth that could make him crawl. "They haven't invented one of them yet, sorry I don't do that shit. Can you imagine, a man getting broken up over a woman, get a fuckin' life pal." She wrecked him. His first time out with her had him listening to her every word. It was amazing, he actually shut his mouth which always ran on, usually about himself. She didn't talk much but when she did it was interesting. She was very smart, he respected this a lot. The sex was nothing short of amazing. The more time he spent with her, the more he began to change. People began to notice. "Jack, you're not half the asshole you used to be. What's up, change your hairdresser?" Well to make a long story short...and you knew this was coming, like I'm really going to let you off the hook with a story about a guy who is not all that bad to start with, who gets stronger and better thanks to the affection and attention of a beautiful young woman. You want fiction? Go shove a 2x4 up your ass and I'll get you a date with Ozzy Osbourne. Ok, now that's fiction. Now back to the real world....This hatchet throwing, glue sniffing car thief. This psychotic schizophrenic nymphomaniac bitch. She broke his heart. He found out that the whole time he thought that he had found the ultimate woman, she was fucking me. Whoa! He got mad too! He came by my house to kick my ass or do some kind of Errol Flynn macho bullshit like that. You're damn right he got shot. What do you think this is, get the fuck out of here.

#61: He was talking to some new guy who was scared shitless. The new guy was talking dust his mouth was so dry, he couldn't seem to catch his breath. He talked in small bursts about home and Jimi Hendrix. They came under fire as fast as an eye blink. The new guy's head exploded, his brains flew and hit him in the face. Warm. Warmth christ mother don't let them kill me. He came home with problems. When he is in open spaces he freaks out, when he is in small spaces he freaks out. He can't sleep for more than a few hours at a time. He looks older than his i.d. He is a walking Death card. He can't drive. He drinks. He shakes for hours at at time. He can't talk to his father and believe me he's tried. He figured his father would understand having seen war in Germany, but it's not even close. He looks into his father's eyes and he's alone. That new guy's brains smelled sweet, they were warm, he remembers the warmth. He shot himself to make the dreams stop.

#62: He pulled up to the red light. Looked over at a man who sat slumped on a bus stop bench. He said "Hey buddy, want a ride?" The man looked up, startled and shook his head no. "Well that's cool, suck on this anyway." The man in the car shot the man on the bench twice in the stomach. The light turned green, the man drove off.

#63: He sat in his room. He thought about women sex killing some motherfucker the job killing the boss because he talked a lot of shit killing every fucking punk he could get in his scope getting the hell out of this town meeting someone he could talk to loneliness the rent the heat the next shift his life should he kill himself and how should he do it the woman he saw at the bus stop what would he say to her if she was here right now hi how are you what's your name no I'm not crazy no I only breathe like this because I have a deviated septum sounds like I'm snorkeling I know ha ha what are you doing tonight oh yea I'm pretty busy too I was just wondering if you were as busy as I was ha ha you know how it is well it was nice meeting you maybe I will run over you again sometime get it I said run over you instead of run into you yea it's a joke ha ha yea I'm a funny one ha ha yea well good bye fuck you too like I really give a fuck what's on your mind if I had wanted to know that I would've asked you wouldn't I yea you're fucking right I would have you know all you bitches are all the same fucking ball breakers all of you yea that's why you get raped that's why your jaws get broken some men don't take your shit they take what they want when they want they are take charge guys like me yea like me yea I rape all the time and you fuck for money all the time what's the difference if I took you out to a nice place to eat if I spent the big money on you then you would give it up you would have to because that's the way the game works and you're a whore don't think you're not and you get raped all the time even in your dreams I know I'm yelling I'll yell anytime

I want to what the fuck did you say well yea go sit on your boyfriend's face until it falls out hey I said I was sorry I don't know what to say to women I get nervous can't you understand how it would be for a guy to see a beautiful woman and want to talk to her but not know what to say but know that he wanted to say something that he had to say something well I just lost my cool for a second there please come back I won't hurt you I can only hurt myself doctors orders ha ha be nice to me and I won't kill myself right here right now ha ha I'm depending on you ha ha the boss what a fucker fat piece of shit the fucker on the bus shouldn't of looked at me like that he doesn't know how close he came to getting himself mutilated like I care about messing some guy's face up the bastards turned off the phone like anyone calls here anyway what a joke the rent the smell of this place killing strangers for no reason I want to die in my sleep the only way I can redeem my self respect is to kill my father and mother knife all the boyfriends the shame I wish I could meet someone that understands me I want someone to know me no one knows me they never will because they're creeps I'm glad to be alone better that way what time is it work starts soon haven't slept yet.

#64: Sometimes I see myself as some kind of superhero. I like to close my eyes and imagine myself with a machine gun running thru the neighborhood killing everyone I see. I can see myself setting houses on fire as I run down the street. I live in my head, it's the only place I can go where everybody knows me. When I look out the window and see all the scum out there, the assholes across the street selling drugs all night long, talking so much shit so loud that I can't sleep. All the noise makes me want to play god. Some asshole outside my window right now screaming that he's going to fuck someone up. I want to burn the kids right in front of their parents, serve them up to the homeless. God does it all the time.

#65: The gunshots were barely audible over the volume of the set. He was watching mtv. He counted the shots and listened for return fire, there was none. Probably someone airing out a new piece or maybe just letting every one know that he had one. He watched the mtv, some man with a lot of make up and teased up hair sang an ode to a "sweet little pleaser." Last week there was a real cool one. A bullet ricocheted and buzzed by his house when he was sitting on the front porch. Sounded like a piece of cloth being torn. He thought that it would be fun to see a man on mtv get shot during a video, to see some rockstar faggot running up a street with his guitar blazing. He stops to get on a bench to solo and look all street tough and shit and out of nowhere a carload of Crips drive by and cap him and the video ends. He thought about how great it would be to shoot one of those fucked up police choppers out of the sky.

#66: A dick thing: She promised to call me after she got back from her trip. I waited for her because I wanted to see her badly and was looking forward to it. 10 days after her supposed return to the country she still hadn't called. Now if she was blowing me off, she could have at least had the guts to have called and told me. I call a few numbers looking for her. Finally I reach her, she seems surprised to hear from me. I ask her why she didn't call me. She gives me some bullshit answer. I know this girl very well, I have known her for years and I know when she's lying. She is not good at it either. So I have a little fun and ask her some rapid fire questions about things that she should be able to tell me immediately. She can't get answers very quickly, of course she can't, she's making them all up as she goes. Being insulted hurts, especially when it's over the phone. Have you ever felt as powerless as when you're trying to deal with something like this over the phone? I know! It makes you crazy. So we finally agree to meet at a restaurant, we can't meet at her new place because "it's being painted." That's nice that her new man is painting the place for her. This is days away from now. I called her later this evening to try to talk to her because it was getting impossible for me to get anything done around here. I called and got a nice deep male voice on the answering machine. Now I don't get into revenge and all this heated passion bullshit, but you know sooner or later I will run into the two of them and it doesn't matter how big or tough this guy is. Chances are he isn't as fucked up crazy and as ready to die as I am. If he is, well all the better. I want her to see me mutilate this guy for the fun of it and also so she can have a good horror story to tell her children years from now. Hell, I'm not even interested in trying to get her to be with me again. I just want to hurt this guy because I know it will hurt her and it will make me feel good. It's a dick thing so you've got to understand!

#67: She came home from the job. Her husband was beating the living shit out of their son. She walked past them, got a beer sat down and watched tv.

#68: I pulled into a 7-11 in Silverlake. A man was standing in front. He had a rag in his hand and he asked me if he could do the windshield. I told him that it was already clean. He said that he needed money. He pointed to his right eye which was caked with blood. "Somebody jacked me." He pointed to a small bundle on top of a Val-U-Vend water dispenser. "That's all my clothes right there." I gave him a dollar and went inside. Two young men were assaulting the video machines. The two men behind the counter were looking at each other perhaps hoping that the other would take the initiative to tell them to stop it. After I bought my stuff. I went out and saw that the window man had found employment cleaning the windshield of a Cadillac. He was singing. "I can see clearly now the rain has come, I can see all obstacles in OUR way."

#69: When he found out how things really were between men and women he found that he had been full of shit for years. It was a drag to find out that everybody knew all the same shit and everyone played it off like it was nothing. All the things that go unsaid, don't go unsaid. They get shoved into your guts like knives. All the bullshit sex etiquette, it was like a miniature cold war. What a bunch of lies and ego trips! That's why all these people were so freaked out about each other. It was one big club. The Look Away and Laugh Club. A revelation the size of this one sent him reeling for the coffee pot. He spent the rest of the day playing watery college radio pop music like the Complacents, No Means No Good and Chokeme Withcock. He scribbled furiously in his note pad about the injustices of the world and he felt very heavy and important.

#70: He would go to those dances. He could never get the nerve to ask a girl to dance. Like he would really know what to do when he got out on the floor. He had tried dancing alone in his room and had gotten so embarrassed that he just had to stop. He watched them though, if you could get points for being attentive he would have cleaned up. Women were so mysterious and full of shit, he wouldn't have a clue what to say to one if he ever got the chance. The dances went by and he went to almost all of them. He would find the darkest part of the gym and watch them with his back to the wall. He saw a girl that was doing the same thing as he was. He checked her out, she was pretty enough. A few times she caught him looking, she was looking at him too after all. He looked at her again and she waved at him. His entire body shuddered. He knew what he should do and at the same time he knew he didn't have the balls to go over and say hello. He was so shy he could barely answer to roll call in class. He looked down at the floor trying to appear unconcerned and even bored. When he looked up again she was there in front of him. His heart started pounding, he thought he might choke. She introduced herself, he managed to get his name out as well. They both agreed that these things were stupid and that they were both there to see how stupid their friends could be and how stupid it was to dance etc. They decided to try it as a joke, you know, like "here eat this pound of lard, but only as a joke though." They went for it in the dark corner of the gym. It was a slow song, something by Three Dog Night. The singer shouted over the music "Look at this, we have all the boys against one wall and the girls against the other, why can't you all be like THOSE TWO OVER IN THE CORNER?!!" He felt his dinner rising up. They broke apart. She ran off. He never saw her again.

#71: He liked her because he could see her deep-seeded hatred for men. Every time they had sex, he thought himself some kind of slick con-man, managing to talk his way into her skirt and get to the booty. He felt like a safe cracker. He thought that he had her right where he wanted her. He couldn't have been more off the mark. He never bothered to ask her what she saw in him. She was an honest person and she would have told him to his face that she thought he was a jerk who knew how to fuck well and that was it. After he left in the mornings or late at night which was his favorite time, she never thought about him at all until he called a few days later to see how his "special little lady" was doing. I like it when people use each other, it's one of the only instances they get to the truth for any sustained period of time.

#72: He got into a lot of fights. He had a temper that wouldn't quit. Violence always made sense. He used to say that a broken nose was the universal language. The more he had to deal with people the more he wanted to fuck them up. It was the only thing he could think to do, like you can really talk to any of these people. They all needed to get their ass kicked. He was a fighting machine. Punching out boyfriends of ex-girlfriends, people that looked at him for too long, you name it and he would fight it. His best move was to come right over, say nothing and start slugging. No one could take that. What the hell are you going to do with a guy that doesn't talk, gets in your face and starts punching it off. Right, so our hero got shot four times in the stomach in a Tom's Burger stand a few weeks ago. The guy who shot him had quite a temper. Homicide had always made sense to him. He would say that there wasn't a problem in the world that couldn't be solved by shooting someone in the face. You just had to find the right person, hell you didn't even need to do that, sometimes just shooting the person next to him was enough. You're so fine, I can't get enough. I want to do it with you all night long. Even though you left me and never told me why, I will always love you because I know you need someone out there to watch over you. It's me, I'll always be there for you even though you might never know where that warm surge of strength running down and spreading across your back is coming from. My thoughts guard you forever.

#73: Every day was a step closer to the gun. Everything he saw told him this. Her hollow expression when she looked at him, the blank eyes that looked at him from the mirror. His total lack of desire for sex. One day at work every face in the office turned into his father's. He saw it all. He had believed too much. It was like a car wreck that took 15 years to stop rolling across the black top. The fire leaving scars, wounds that turned his dreams to self destructive rages, turned life into an unblinking endless grey process of seeing it seeing it seeing it. He got up from his desk and went home. He shot his wife twice in head, shot his daughter and shot himself. You will never out live the damage done by the mother and the father, even if you never knew them. They still scar you. It's all damage. Everything burns and mutilates. Life is terrifying. Ascend. Respect yourself. Embrace true power. Explore the number One. Taste Death. Do not fear life's lie.

#74: He had it all wrong. His big downfall was that he thought he had women figured out. Any man that tells you he has women figured out is full of shit. He would come over to her house, eat her food, fuck, shower and leave. He thought it was the Life of Riley, the sport of kings. One afternoon when he was over there trying to pull her clothes off so he could get a fast one before he went to work, she pushed him off and told him he had it all wrong. This wasn't a 7-11 in her pants. He punched her in the side of her head and told her to shut the fuck up he would take what he wanted when he wanted to. They got married 3 months later.

#75: He kept to himself. People made him feel bad. It was nothing they could help. He didn't hold it against them, he took it as fact. He spent a lot of time alone in his room. It's where he felt best. He stared at the walls and tried not to think too much. The problem with his thoughts was that they always involved them, always them. In his English class they had to write a short paragraph expressing themselves. Every one in the class had to read theirs out loud. His went like this: You have to get away from them. You have to get as far away as you can otherwise they'll kill you with their lives. They don't know what they do. They are careless with themselves and they take too much for granted. They make their shortcomings your problem. The only way to keep your head above it and heal your wounds is to crawl away.

#76: When the depression hit him it felt like a stone had been dropped on his soul. He couldn't tell anyone about it. He tried to tell a girl about it once when they were riding on a bus. She had nodded her head and said that she sometimes got depressed but she had little time for that kind of thing. She said that you only get depressed if you have nothing better to do. It was obvious that she didn't know where he was at. He got it so bad sometimes that he wasn't capable of anything. He would shut down. One day he sat in his chair and stared at the ground for 7 hours without getting up. He started to make jokes to himself about the depression. He gave it a name, might as well, it was over at the house often enough. As he got older the depression would come more frequently, hit harder and stay longer. He became more withdrawn. It got to the point to where he could barely speak. He knew he was totally alone in the world. Sometimes he would wake up in the middle of the night and want to die. He would stare at the blackness of the room and want to end it all right then. Life hurt so much at times it was unbearable. He knew that he wasn't going to make it to old age.

#77: They lived together. The apartment was small and poorly lit. At first things were ok between them. It was the first time that either of them had lived with their lover so there was that nervous enthusiasm that goes with all of that bullshit. It took a few months but things started to fall apart. At night he would go for long walks to get some time to himself. He would come back and she would give him a bunch of shit because she thought he was meeting with someone else. He told her that she could follow him anytime provided that she kept her distance behind him. He just wanted some space that's all. Finally the lease was up. They hated each other's guts and they moved to opposite sides of the city and never saw each other. I'll never do that again, it was one of the worse times of my life. She had me putting up curtains. Hell, I did it! What a sell-out. What the fuck is it about laundromats? When you go in there with your mate, you always come out of there in some kind of seething argument. Happened to me every time. It was easier to sneak out with the clothes and do the damn wash alone and not deal with all the petty bullshit.

You could go in there at any time of the week and there would be a couple in there staring furiously at magazines, or watching the dryer like television. Hating each other's guts. I'd rather live alone.

#78: A man walks. He walks for days. Occasionally he stops to eat. He sleeps a few hours and rises before dawn. He walks, he talks to no one. He never stops moving if he can help it. People pull to the side of the road and ask if he needs a ride. He says nothing and keeps walking. He doesn't think. He is finished with thinking. They will not like what you think. Where are your friends when the shit comes down? Right. All there is, is you. You are number one. Build a fire, lock and load. This trip is for real. Fuck them. If you listen to them for too long you'll become them. You have to go until the flesh falls away.

#79: I wait in this room for the world to start. I wait for some kind of signal to tell me how I'm going to get thru this age of cheap cruelty. I'm waiting for the incinerating light. I think I'll know it when it comes and I'll know what to do. It's a hard time. I think hard words are in order. Am I all alone in this? Are the only hard words the ones from my mouth alone? Why do they shun me? Why am I driven to my room to wait? Where is the world? Will I know it when I meet it and will its blood taste different than mine?

#80: They were married in the fall. 6 months later he shot himself in the head. Her grief is beyond belief. She wants to die all the time. A cancer has been let loose inside her. When the sun sets over the Pacific and the sound of the traffic makes the windows of the apartment shake. She cries. She sleeps on the floor, she cannot face the bed. She has thought about smelling the pillow where his head lay so she could remember. 5 days ago he was there. It's hard to go on.

#81: The heat makes monsters come from out of her mouth. Two headed, three headed, how many monsters do you want? How much evil do you need? Do you need a tool to inflict evil upon yourself with more ease? Turn the lights on. The heat makes her hit things. The heat makes the spirits come from out of the bottle. The dreams come back. Her father comes back from the dead to strike fear again like he never left. She is swinging from a vine in her brain, she is the master killer. The heat takes all of the heat out of the room. When is it real and when is it illusion? Is she the eternal whore or the rodent behind the wall? How much heat can she eat. We wait for you. We will get you and keep getting you. Napalm keeps burning in your head.

#82: He tries to talk to her. Words fail him miserably. They choke him in mid-sentence. His hands take flight. The more he tries to talk the worse it gets. She looks at him like he's crazy. He tries to relax but it's no use, nothing comes out at all. She asks him what his problem is. He wants to hide. He wants to scream, he wants to explode. Please don't let me scare you. I can't talk, no one touches me, you're so beautiful, no one knows me. Please don't leave. I am so lonely. She looks at him. He looks like someone trying to breathe for the first time in years.

#83: I was going to shoot her in her living room. I knew it. I had it all in my head. Earlier that morning I had been there and I had picked up the rest of my stuff. I felt like an asshole picking up my shit and putting it in a plastic bag while she watched like some mother. I could see that she didn't really want me to go. Perfect, keep them hanging on so you can hurt them later. If they forgive you once they'll keep forgiving you, you can do any damn thing you want with them. This woman pissed me off. I thought I was above falling love. I was always the player, the mind fucker. I was damn good at it too. I used to take a real pride in seeing how far I could take these stupid bitches. I loved seeing them cry. This morning it was me who had been the one crying. I asked her how she could turn me away like this. I figured I would plant the guilt seed in her tiny mind so I could rake her thru the coals later on. I could see it almost work. She tried to stay strong "Why don't you grow up and be a man for once in your life, cut out the dramatics." I felt my whole body tense. I was going to break her neck right there but that would be too easy. In this life I strive for control at all times. She almost made me lose it all. I'll admit it, I loved her. Hours later I was on my way back to her place with my gun in my pants. I got to her place and knocked on the door. She didn't open it up but instead pushed the mail slot open and told me that she was busy and would call me later. So busy that she couldn't open the door, what the fuck was going on in there? I told her to open up, I wanted to give her something. She told me to put it in thru the slot. I said ok. I opened up the slot and looked in. She was standing right in front of me. I shoved the barrel of the gun in the slot and fired 3 times. I hit her in the stomach at least twice. I turned and split. I walked back down her street towards Sunset Blvd. I felt nothing. I passed an apartment complex. There was a man standing in front of the small pool right by the fence. I stopped and stared at him. I don't know why. Finally he smiled and said "Hello, my name is Paul." I took the gun out of my pants and shot him in the stomach. He fell to the ground. I walked away. I didn't run. I don't know why. I don't remember feeling anything. I went home, made some dinner, played some records and fell asleep. I went to work the next day and that was it. That was six months ago.

#84: I live alone in my room. I don't talk to anyone not even at work. I work in a basement, I know what to do. I spend as much time as I can in my room alone. The more time I spend alone, the more I want to. It's like a disease. I am drawn to myself yet at the same time I am sickened and repulsed. I never speak. I hate the sound of my voice. I don't have a phone, I don't want to hear anyone say my name. I'm trying to forget I have one. If I don't think about myself enough maybe I will forget that I am. When I eat food I try not to taste it. I don't want to know what keeps me alive. I expel as much information as I can from my head in hopes that I will forget it forever. My bodily functions disgust me. I hate it when I see hair growing on my face. The less I am the better. I am a blackout drinker. In the darkness I forget myself in hopes that sometime I will not remember my life. I have totally blanked out all memories of my mother and father. In my mind I have turned them into an impossibility. I know that I am from nothing, no one. The less I am the better. I want to be nothing.

#85: They had done it like 5 or 6 times. Every time it felt the same to him. She was beautiful and sex with her was good, but like all the other women he had been with after it was over for the night he felt nothing for them. He would forget to call them back after a few days. He would hear people talking about how they were so close to the one they loved. He didn't know what the hell they were talking about. He had never loved anyone in his life. Mother, father, no one.

He spent an evening at her apartment. They ended up in bed. An hour later he was in the shower. He put on his clothes and took off saying he would call her. He always did shit like that and he didn't know why. He felt like someone had pulled a string in his back.

The next evening she called him and said she wanted to come

over. She showed up an hour later. He stabbed her four times in the chest and blacked out.

He is in a max security ward in Northern Cal. He said in an interview that he has forgiven himself and that's all that matters. It's what you think of yourself. No one can judge you and be right. No one knows you. You do what you do and that's it.

#86: All his life he believed everything his father told him. Now he's in his mid-thirties and he's his own man. He hates his father's guts but no longer fears him. He never said NO to the fucker even he was humiliating him in front of his friends. Now he works extra hard to raise his self respect. It has taken him years to find out who he is. Years spent trying to wash the father blood from his body. He's earned his life. It's funny how people think that they have "a right to life." Now isn't that the biggest load of shit you ever heard? You don't have a right to shit your pants on Sunday. Let's take it back to the jungle. Where the fuck are your rights there? No lawyers in the jungle. Civilization has allowed the weak to survive. You can sit back like an overweight apathetic piece of shit and smoke your dope and still survive because you have a right to life. The gang-bangers I saw getting rousted up the street from here, on their knees with their hands over their heads. The pigs with their guns in their faces screaming at them, they have a right to life? You should have the seen the pigs' guns reflecting in their flashlight beams. Sit in your chair and talk your shit about your right to life when a pig has his gun in your eye. You can go out and buy the same kind of a gun a pig carries. You can do that. When you shoot a pig, go for a head shot. The little shits are all wearing vests now, all you would do is break a rib or two.

#87: She shoots junk, she never had to tell so many lies in her life. It's no big thing anymore, she does what she has to do to get by.

A few years ago when she was living in the Midwest you couldn't have made her believe she was going to fuck guys she didn't know for a dose of smack. It's funny how things change. You know, you always have to be ready to change. Adapt or perish. That's good to keep in mind while some pig is beating the shit out of you. That'll get you thru the nights of sucking dick on Santa Monica Blvd. To go from human to mutant is to learn to live in the city. Embrace the disease or go back to the Midwest.

#88: I am a pounded piece of paper. Flat and tasteless. They tell me that I am something. I nod my head that I understand. I understand that it's just you and me in this room and that all of this comes to nothing. That's our secret. It's our Death writ. 1-2-3 implode. Slow backward flame. You in your room and me in mine.

#89: We follow a man all over the world. He goes from one phone booth to another. We see a look of pain and fatigue on his face as the years go by. He goes from airplane to camel back. Ferryboat to hydrofoil. Always the phone is waiting for him. We never hear what he's hearing, we never see who is calling. It's all in his face. He gets a call in Cairo. He flies to LA. He gets in a taxi. He gets out in front of a house and there's a woman standing on the grass in front of the porch. They embrace. She pulls out a knife and stabs him deeply and violently in the stomach. He folds on the lawn and it looks like he's done for. She leaves. He gets up and pulls off the flack vest he was wearing and throws it on the porch as he walks briskly away to a phone that's ringing.

#90: The nights were hot and memorable. The sex was beyond belief. She was the answer to everything. All the questions he ever had as to why he should live at all were in her eyes. That was the last summer he ever saw outside of prison.

#91: They took him underneath the stairs. He pleaded with them. One of them punched him in the mouth and told him that he was going to die if he didn't do what they told him to. He sucked all their dicks. They beat the shit out of him and left. He vomited and somehow got home. It was his fourth week as a police officer. He was found a month later under the same place with a screwdriver in the side of his head and his severed cock in his mouth. He was one of 13 pigs that were killed in that county that summer. No one was ever caught.

#92: He stood behind her for the better part of an hour. She barely moved. It was as if the television had some kind of magic hold on her. He watched the back of her greying head as it gently nodded with the canned laughter. It was the end of all time. It was the end of all struggle and all sorrow. No more lying awake at night thinking about the job and money. Numbers! How many hundreds of hours had he wasted thinking about money and little numbers in little rows so nice and neat. Numbers weren't anything! What a revelation so late in the game. What was real life anyway? Did he ever really live? Was there ever a moment when he wasn't in fear of losing something? Had he wasted his life away? He thought about the lines in his face. 64 years, was that old? Too late to start over again. He would look at all the women on the street and know that it was too late to even think about doing anything. He looked down at her head. He called her name out loud. "Ellen." She jumped slightly and turned around in time to see him shoot himself in the mouth. It was the end of time.

#93: She was like you, she was getting older by the minute. In the morning she would look into the mirror trying to see if the night had stolen anything from her face. She looked closely at the lines around her eyes and mouth. "Not bad for 34" she said to herself.

She knew she looked better a few years ago. There had been a time when her face did not change appearance for years and she thought she would look that way forever. She couldn't pinpoint exactly when her face fell into that adult serious semi-scowl. She would stare at the younger girls at work and distract herself. "I should have gotten married when I was still attractive" she said out loud. She listened to the lightness of their talk, sounded like a bunch of children talking about nothing. She stared at her hands. She never knew how to deal with her body. Her few fleeting relationships with men had made her shy and self-conscious. A man had told her that she was lifeless and bad in bed. She would spend the weekends alone. She had no interest in music, she never read books or newspapers. She had no friends to call. She had not the slightest idea of how to meet a man. She was scared of bars, she felt discomfort to the point of panic upon entering. She always thought that someone was going to see that she didn't belong there and tell her to get the hell out. She wouldn't know what to order anyway. The younger girls made it all look so easy. She wondered if they ever went thru the hours of self-hatred and self-doubt that scarred her waking hours. She wondered if they were ashamed of their bodies the way she was. Sometimes she hated them. When she saw young women with men on the street going somewhere, she looked to see if she could put herself in the woman's place. It was a different language that they were speaking. She didn't understand. Sometimes the lines in her face felt very deep. A life time of loneliness and uncertainty.

#94: He was driving home from work in medium traffic. He had the radio on to balance out the roar of the wind thru the window. He looked at the steering wheel, there was a fly perched between his hands. With his right hand he tried to swat the fly. The fly easily dodged his hand, circled his head and landed on the tip of his nose. He smacked himself on the face and cursed. The car in the next lane beeped as he swerved. The fly was now perched on his left hand. He didn't try to hit it. He just watched it as it rubbed its front legs together. He made a grab at the fly and missed. He hit an abandoned car at over 70 miles an hour. The car burst into flames and exploded. The man was destroyed, the fly flew away.

#95: The story of a genius: He was drunk in a rough bar. He started talking shit. A bouncer took him outside and beat the hell out of him. He got home and vomited blood and scotch all over the rug by his front door. He thought about going back to the place and kicking that guy's ass. He thought about it some more and thought that it might be better if he just stayed home and took it easy. That's what he did. Genius.

#96: And finally after much waiting and contractual litigation, all the Los Angeles county pigs and their families were shot in the face and everybody lived happily ever after.

#97: He loved her completely. Even when she was ignoring his ass, even when she was fucking someone else and calling him up to tell him how good it was. After long periods of writing her letters and calling her and getting humiliated, he started to hate her. He started to get in a lot of fights. He spent a lot of time alone. He worked overtime so he would have something to do. He was an artist, he could turn his hands into fists. Like magic, like a big black night, like battery acid. Like life with a hole in one of its tires. She was beautiful and out of reach. He needed a song, he needed something to talk to him. He counted the days that he didn't call her. He thought of her all the time. No one is worth all that bullshit. People are fucked. They fill your life with pain. Every time you think it'll be different it's not. It's always the same bag of lying evil shit. When they get killed on the freeway, they ought to let you stand on the bodies and get your picture taken to give you something to smile about. Long live Black Sabbath!

#98: His father told him to come into the bathroom. He went, he always did what he was told. He never said no to his father. His father told him to take his clothes off because they were going to take a shower. He had never seen his father's cock before. It was much bigger than his was and very hairy. His father took the boy's hand and put it on his cock. The boy didn't know what he was supposed to do, he involuntarily shuddered. When he did something wrong, or forgot something he was taught, he was punished with a slap to the head. He wondered if they had gone over this before. He told the boy to open his mouth. His father put his cock in the boy's mouth. Before he really knew what was going on, his father pulled back and slapped him hard across the face. The boy fell and struck his head hard on the faucet. Father told the boy to get up and get dressed and ready for dinner. Stepmother would be home soon.

#99: At this point you have found the note and you have found my body as well. In the envelope with this letter, please find 300 dollars in cash. That should cover the cost of cleaning the room of the mess that I have now made of it. I think there's a cleaning company that specializes in getting blood and gunpowder out of rugs and walls. Check the Yellow Pages. There should be some money left in my account please use it to dispose of the body. Anything that's leftover please pay any outstanding bills that come up in the next few weeks. I know what you're thinking. If he's dead, why the hell would he care if the bills are paid or not? Well I do care, I might as well be responsible for all of this shit. You should have seen me here wracking my brains (ha ha!) trying to find a way to kill myself and dispose of the body at the same time. I mean, shit, I would not like to be looking at the scene that you are. Sorry, I tried to do something with a little bit more style and flair but at the time, my mind was troubled, now it's all over the room, ha ha.

I suppose you want to know why I did it. I couldn't find anything that meant anything to me. Money, women, sex, love, fame, friends, none of that could hold me. I think it's all a bunch of shit. So much lying involved to get any of it happening anyway. When was the last time you got a date with a girl and didn't lie every 5 minutes? Right, well I got tired of the lies. If you tell the truth too much, you'll go broke!

At the job I felt like a fucking robot, I can't believe I stuck with it so long in the first place. Isn't it the stupidest damn thing you can think of to do with your time? Get up and get dressed and go there to take it from some asshole. Go back home and get ready to do it all over again the next day? Not me, not anymore. Look at all of our friends, if you can call them that. The only time they're not bitching is when they have just found a new way to fuck someone over. Otherwise they're the same predictable mean-assed bunch, just like all the others. I don't mean to come on all heavy and shit but I felt like a hamster in a cage. Running for the food, hitting the treadmill every day. It was an insult that I could no longer stand. The things that I considered "good," good torture is what it was, good sado-masochism. Nothing more. Life is Death in slow motion. It takes years. They give you the poison so slowly you can't even taste it. So look, don't get all bummed out with this ok? I am where I should be. It was coming to this. I saw this coming years ago. It was just a matter of time until I got the courage up to give up the poison. I don't want you to feel that you have to do this. If you can deal with life's bullshit parade, then more power to you.

Again, sorry for the mess.

#100: It was late. They were in bed, yes they were doing it. Would I waste your time telling a story about two people sleeping? That would be a real killer: They lay there, they breathed in, they breathed out, dawn was approaching ....Right, go talk to Andy Warhol. The best thing he ever did was take that mutant Grace Jones for a lot of money. Too bad he didn't take her out of circulation for keeps. Ok, do you remember the white guy in the movie "48 Hours"? He talked about giving his woman "the high hard one." Isn't that gross? Who writes this shit? Anyway, that's what this guy was doing with this girl.

They were having a good old time, making all the party noises and doing all that adult bedtime shit. The phone rings. It's 3:00 in the morning and the phone rings, what the fuck. She picks it up. Think about that, he's on top of her and she reaches over and picks up the phone. How the hell would you like to be that guy? All hot and bothered, frozen in the ridiculous push-up position trying to look nonchalant. Checking out the walls, too dark to see the shitty paintings. It would be no easy deal striking the pose and trying to maintain an erection. So to amuse yourself you listen to the conversation and as a joke you stick it in with great emphasis to see if you can make her talk funny like when you stick a red hot poker up someone's ass while they're saying grace. So you do that and she makes a face like a snake and you make some kind of face like "Like shucks, can't this phone call wait until morning?""But it comes out looking like "Get the fuck off the phone, I'll have you now!" That makes her mad. So you start to pull out and she grabs your shoulder like "Don't go!" and you think to yourself that this must mean that she'll be off soon. Meanwhile you're getting bored with all this sex business and you start to think of all the stupid shit you've done in the past to get laid. You start to feel like a jerk for making such a big deal about something that is admittedly great but not worth some of the idiotic positions you have found yourself in like this one here. Then your mind starts to drift to the pressing shit that you got together with the girl to temporarily leave behind: Taxes, old age, Death, your weight, your job, life's uselessness and why are we here and is there life on other planets and you have to be at work in 6 hours. So what the hell is she talking about? It's easy to tell that it's an old boyfriend. It's getting tense and she's raising her voice and you figure maybe it's a good time to pull out and take that piss that you have been thinking about for the last 10 minutes. So you're pulling out and she pulls you back really hard and starts to bang on your head and shoulder for emphasis while talking to this guy who you don't hate but are starting to get a mild distaste for. She starts to cry, your erection is really shriveling up now. It falls out of her body with a sad and barely audible "pop." Now you're cramping and you're sore. You can tell by her voice that she's really into this guy and it doesn't really matter to you all that much but it does. Now she's yelling at the guy and you start to feel like a total stranger. You feel like you're 15 again. That time when you made out for 5 hours straight and then went home and your balls felt like they had been run over by a tank. There's a cold thing next to your leg, it's your other leg that has been asleep for who knows how long. It feels like a side of beef. You are afraid to touch it. From 1000 miles away you hear her hang up. Like the fool you are, you the one with his dick in park for the last millennium, you come up with this great one liner: "So where were we?" all sexy and shit like she can even remember your name in the first place. She looks at you like you just asked her of she would like a live swordfish stuck up her ass. "How can you think of sex at a time like this?" It takes awhile but soon you're back to what you were doing before the phone call and at this point it's just to say that you did it. You go at it with the head down grimace of the working man. You're right about to come and the phone rings again. She speaks for a few minutes and hangs up. She looks up at you and says that you'll have to leave. He's coming over. She asks you to kindly remove yourself from her which you do. She shakes your hand and says that it was really nice meeting you and could please put your clothes on and split before he gets here. She gets up and starts changing the sheets. You ask why the hell she's doing that, they're clean as can be, nothing happened in them. She says that Walter doesn't like this pattern. You leave without another word. You're standing out in hallway and you get this great idea. You take a long look up and down the hallway and the coast is clear. You pull out your pud and beat off all over the doorstep in hopes that maybe, just maybe, Walter will slip on it and break his goddamn neck. Good night.

#101: He felt ripped off. Like some part of his life had been denied him by some ugly and unseen twist of fate. He was almost 30 and he knew there was no chance. All his life he had wanted romance and he knew that it was never going happen. He was going bald, he thought about killing himself when he first noticed it. He wanted to meet a girl and fall in love. He knew that it only happened to kids in high school and that was well behind him. The diamonds of his mind has been stolen by ugly hands. All things had turned to brass and tin. He lived alone, he listened to a lot of that old punk rock shit, old soul and 70's music. It made him remember the places he had been near but had never quite gotten to. After a certain age you can't go back, you've seen too much and experience becomes an enemy. These teenagers had no idea what they had going for them. He could taste the tin in his mouth. Do you ever feel regret? All the things you could have done without risking getting shot in the mouth like these days? Without getting hopelessly in debt. Do you ever look around and see the world as a thief that steals from you and forces you into being a loser with a stupid grin on your face? Do you ever count all the times you have denied all the things you feel so you wouldn't have to do anything about them? Our boy shuffled into middle age silently and without protest.

#102: Life's kiss of Death! Death was everywhere. It was in everything that he saw around him. Life's hollow expression and cold touch, life's uncaring kiss. One morning he woke up and all he could think of was that he had been destroyed by his parents and it was too late to change. They had taken him like a con man takes a drunk sailor. He had believed too much. It was the grind that finally got to him, never getting any farther than the men's room. Life had a bad draft, the lights were poor and it smelled like a toilet. His single room smelled like a bar. Old smoke and stale beer crowded his dreams and pushed him around. This was his life, everywhere in the world was Long Beach California. He didn't kid himself, he knew damn well he was never getting out of there unless he shot himself and all that was was another thought to trip on during happy hour.

#103: August. There's a man in an apartment, he's sweating and out of his mind. He spreads the classified section on the kitchen and goes into the living room. He picks a baby up out of a crib that's in the corner and takes it over to the sink. He takes its diaper off and runs the kid under cold water. He places the crying child on the paper. He takes a knife and hacks the kid into fist-sized hunks. He takes the whole thing to the window and throws it out. It lands on the sidewalk. He looks down at all the people freaking out and staring back up at him. He closes the window, washes his hands and goes back to the television which is always on.

#104: She was outside the liquor store every time I went in. She always had her kid with her. She would panhandle for money by telling people that she was trying to feed it. It worked, I gave her money all the time. Maybe the kid would grow up and shoot her for making him breathe in all that shitty LA air. One night a car backed into the kid at about 3 miles an hour and killed it. I hear she's still out there but now she just sits on a milk crate with her hand out and says nothing.

#105: They called her "The Throw Away Girl." People tried to talk to her and all they would get is a steady and relentless stream of abuse in return. She was great, she destroyed them regularly. She would cut them to pieces, it was great to see her shove men right up their ass and make you laugh at the same time she made you think. She liked me because she said that we both hated everything and knew that friendship was an act of desperation. She said that for a man I was alright. She said that people were "half-way" and if it was up to her a lot of people would get killed and a lot of men would be walking around without their balls. She said that testicles should go on sale for women to hang off their rear view mirrors. She got married and has 3 kids now. She gained a lot of weight and calls everybody her friend. What happens to these people.

#106: He came home to a small room. He worked at a place. At the end of the day he couldn't remember the name of the place. All he knew was that he stood in front of a moving belt and put metal parts into a box. He didn't know what the parts were for. One day he asked the woman that gave him his paycheck what the name of the place was and all she did was laugh and tell him to get the fuck back to work. He didn't push it, he needed the job. He lived alone and never had visitors. He didn't know anyone at work, no one there ever talked to each other. One day he asked the paycheck lady if he was alive and she said no of course not now shut up and get back to work.

#107: His father drank and it scared him. His father would yell and hit his mother. He would hide in his room and wait for it to stop. Now he sits in a cell. His father sits in front of the television set.

#108: At school he was called "The Elephant Man." He was fat and ugly. He wasn't stupid, a lot of people think that goes along with being overweight and not looking like a male model, like people think that beautiful blonde women are air-headed. He was tormented constantly at school. The little pieces of shit would never know his world. Everywhere he went, people freaked out on him. He knew more about people than anyone thought possible. He knew that he was a different animal than they were. He saw how weak and surface level the values a lot of people's entire lives were based upon. Not that this understanding does you any good when you're alone in your room and you're lonely as hell.

#109: The Roach: I wait. Yes in this room I wait for the answer. I need a truth, at this point any one will do. I need to know how the hell I'm going to get thru this age of cruelty. The sun comes up, the sun goes down. I watch them do it each other over and over. I keep expecting to see them blow it up. The humans are well past the point of insanity. Look at them scurry and shriek. These are hard times, I think hard words are in order. Are the hard words for hard times my words alone? Am I the only one that isn't going to run away? Why do they shun me. They are dipped in blood and fear. They walk the pathways of their future graves. They wouldn't know real life if it came thru their window and ripped their teeth out with pliers. For them it's all duck and cover. Now they have me doing it too. I wait, yes in the cracks I wait for incinerating light. My ashes will rip the blinders from your eyes.

#110: Feeling better now that it's all over. That was hard phone call to make. I told her that I don't want to be with her anymore.

If you saw her you would call me crazy. She threw me off, the problem was that she actually liked me and wanted to be close to me. The closer she tried to get, the farther away she would drive me. It's not as if she was all in my shit or anything. She gave me all the space I wanted. If I can't be with her then I can't be with anyone. Anyway, I feel good now that it's over with. All is back to normal. I could never really deal with them. I tried. I'm going for a long walk tonight. I don't want to know anyone, people fill me with loneliness. I live in the city but I'm going to make believe that I live in the desert. The black wind cleaning the thoughts of them from my head, taking the sound of their voices from my ears. I can't get far enough away from them. They cause me so much fucking pain that I want to kill them all just so I won't have to think about them and their lives. I hope I never see that girl again. I shouldn't have messed with a human in the first place. I should have known better.

#111: Dateline Beverly Hills, California: It had been a slow morning at Mega Fake Self Promotion Inc. The head honchos were getting restless, looking for a world to save. Sting called out "Bono, do that one liner from 'Rattle', the one about Charles Manson." Boner leapt on top of a table. He had an annoying habit of climbing on furniture when he spoke. (Face it, he was disgusting. I'm glad he's dead now.) "Right!" cried out Bozo, eyes brimming with tears. "This is a song that Charles Manson stole from the Beatles, and we're stealing from the blacks, I mean we're stealing it back!" Bruce looked up from the floor, a long string of saliva hung from his mouth "Wendy, we're gonna.....I was born ta....demerol....uh...never mind..." He fell off his chair and started moaning something about "searchin' fer somethin'." Bravo looked at the food stains on Bruno's shirt and jeans and wondered to himself if there was any real management left in the world. Stim got on the phone to reception "Jim you simple minded close-set eyed bubble butt mother fucker, get us some coffee and get your bitch to go out to the park and score some of that 'tunnel of love' shit for The Loss before he wakes up and tries to record again." Jim got up off his seat and waddled over to where Chryssie was passed out on the floor. This was the best part of the day. He backed up a couple of steps and kicked her in the behynde as hard as he could, she woke with a start. "Hey I was sleeping you fat fuck!" "Nae ya wurn't, sta pretendin', go score for his highness ya coont." The phone rang. Sling jumped for it only to be edged out by Bolo. "Yes, we're on our way!!" He hung up and jumped up on a chair and shouted down to Sturm "Put your make up on there's a cause on you bitch. Maybe some cute guys too!" "What's the cause, Miss Thing?" "A cat caught in a tree, Winnie Mandela's cat!" Bone-me called into the front office "Hey shit for brains, call our managers and merchandisers, there's a cause on, we're gonna clean up!"

Joe Cole pulled the trigger on the RPG. The grenade went thru the front door and exploded. The building was reduced to rubble, killing all inside. The end, roll credits.

#112: He was in love! Ok, he thought was. He was kind of sure. No he was! When he looked at her he was out of control. She looked better in some settings more than others. There was a few times where he was afraid to take her out. Other times he wanted to show her off like a new car! He wanted to spend the rest of his life with her!! Sometimes he saw other women and he thought about never being able to hit on anyone else again and it made him lose his breath. Then he would think about when he was old, he would need someone to be with him when he wasn't so great looking. But then again all he had to do was go to a movie and see some guy in his 40's with a 19 year old, and he couldn't limit himself to one woman. What if she got fat! Ok he married her, he did not shoot himself in the head.

#113: He spent most of his time in his room. His mother would usually have some man over and they scared the shit out of him. He figured if he stayed in his room and out of the way he wouldn't get thrown out into the street like his mother had threatened to do in the past. He had food stored underneath his bed in case he was booted out. He figured he could take his sleeping bag with him and make it in the park. When he stayed in his room his mother would seem to forget that he was in the apartment. He played his records, he made up people to talk to. At school he didn't fit in, he had no idea how to talk to his classmates. They were black and he was white and to him that made no difference but it did to them. He got punched out regularly. They told him that he had shot Martin Luther King. They called him "cracker." He would get up hours before school started because the fear and anticipation of getting his ass kicked made it impossible for him to sleep. In his room was good though, they all left him alone. He could play the records and sing along. Life seemed tolerable when he was alone. His mother was a shrieking snake witch. His father lived across town and was a source of intimidation and humiliation. He would grow into a strong rage driven monster that rose like an iron sun. If you want to see him in action, stick around. You won't have to wait very long.

#114: He sat in the bar. The happy hour had driven them all into the floor. He listened to them talk and tried to make believe that he wasn't in the same fucked up boat they were. He knew he was though. He was a violent animal like them. They were all addicted to poison and the smell of Death. He saw Death everywhere, they all did. Ever since the war. He lost his wife 8 years ago, had no idea where she was. He had her picture in his wallet but it had been stolen or lost, he hadn't a clue where the fuck it was and he didn't care. You learn to throw things away, thoughts, memories, friends, you learn to lose. The better you get at it the easier it is to get thru life. All life does is take from you. It bleaches your bones and takes your flesh to market. When you try to hold on, pieces of you get torn away. Life was for the young and alive. Ever since he got back he's been walking dead. He could never get the smell of Death from his skin. He saw Death's smiling face on all of his buddies as they sat and waited for it to walk in and order up.

#115: Loneliness is her friend. She lost her job today. The rent is due in two weeks, it's like a bad dream. The night comes, she drinks and wonders what she'll do.

#116: He was 6 years old when he met his father face to face for the first and only time. His father drove down from Buffalo to meet him. He told his son about the times before he and his mother were divorced. The boy looked at him and couldn't imagine this man and his mother together. They ate dinner at some steak place and then went to the parking lot to pick up the car. That was when his father put his hands on him. He rubbed his son's thigh and asked if that was alright. Before he knew what was happening his father was kissing his neck and squeezing his balls. He said "Pull your pants down I want to see how you're growing up." He did. His father put his mouth on his cock. The stubble on his father's face made his leg jerk, hitting his father's nose hard. He lifted his head and told him to pull his pants up. They drove back to his mother's house in silence. When they got to the house he told him to say hello to his mother and it was nice meeting his son. Then he said get the hell out of the car. A coincidence here, both of them died on the same day 15 years later. The father fell asleep at the wheel of his car and smashed into a median embankment and the son hanged himself in the barracks where he was stationed in Germany.

#117: Look, you're bleeding. Did he hit you? Why don't you leave him. What do you mean you owe him money, look you're bleeding again. You know that shit will rot out the middle of your nose. Sorry to hear that you can't get yourself out of this, I guess you have to pay him back. Look you're bleeding. You should watch that shit, you don't look like you used to. I don't mean to get personal but I'm worried about you. I don't understand when you say that you love him, does he love you? I would figure if he did he wouldn't do that to you. Damn, you're bleeding.

#118: So she was fucking Vince again. He was a fat piece of shit and they both knew it. But hey, he had the stuff and that's what she lived for so she didn't mind fucking this piece of human garbage that never washed. He would give her a free fix for a fuck. She thought it was a good deal.

#119: He came home from work. He went into the bathroom. "Good-bye" was written on the mirror in lipstick, like some fucking movie. He walked into the bedroom, all of her clothes and pictures were gone. He could feel his heart pounding in his throat. He left the lipstick on the mirror. He carried the word in his head for months. He could remember with painful detail, every part of her body. The bedroom still smelled of her perfume.

#120: These dudes were sharing a joint in the doorway of an apartment building. A man on his way to work passed them and told them to smoke that shit somewhere else. One of the dudes punched him hard in the face and told him to shut up, they were getting high. The man went back to his apartment and called the police but hung up while the line was still ringing. He was afraid to tell the pigs for fear of the stoners retaliating. He was afraid to do anything to them, he knew they would beat the shit out of him, maybe stab him. He called in sick to work. He vomited in the toilet and crawled back into bed with his suit and tie on.

#121: These guys were beer-bonging at a party. This one guy was shotgunning a beer and didn't know that someone had put bleach in it. He put the beer and bleach right down. He hit the floor and went into convulsions. The guy who did it was 3 blocks away by that time. He did it because he thought the guy had ripped off his brother's surfboard.

#122: He started to slip. He could feel it. Right there at the breakfast table the gleaming doors of madness swung open and sunlight streamed in. He stared into his coffee and listened to the music playing in his head. The vision of the endless beach rolled in front of his eyes, girls in bikinis, helicopters and lots of smoke. Fire, the doors were wide open, the music, the master's voice. War was all there was left, all these years he had denied the facts. They had taken his soul and kept it in the jungle and were waiting for him to come back and get it. He was on his way.

#123: This was a year of change. He must be getting old he thought to himself. He never used the word "bitch" before but now he used it all the time. Hitting her was that last thing that he would ever do. Now he wanted to belt the bitch every time she opened her mouth. She asked him for a drink of water yesterday, a drink of water, big deal. He saw her face falling to the floor. He made his hand into a tool of love: a fist. He pounded her and didn't know it until he was pulling back.

#124: He learned to flinch years ago. Every time his father moved he would flinch. He had been smacked in the head so many times by him that sudden movements would make him flinch and drop things. When he nearly punched out a cashier who handed him a receipt, it was all he could take. He got in his car and drove to his father's house. He hadn't been there in years, in fact he had never driven there himself. It was strange to see the streets go by. It took him back, made him remember the weekend visits. When he got there he found his father mowing the lawn. He got out of the car and ran over to him. He said nothing, he saw his father's face registering surprise and a healthy dose of fear. He sent a beautiful clean left into his father's face. The fist went thru all your father's faces. Thru the face of every cop and kept going.

INVISIBLE WOMAN BLUES

Before I fall asleep at night, I close my eyes and wrap myself around you. I can feel your breath on my neck. In my mind it's real, you're real. Just writing about it makes me stare at the wall for minutes at a time in a trance. Today I sat in a park for hours and wrote hundreds of words to you. I looked up and saw people staring, they're always staring at me, pointing. Trying to pry under my skull, trying to read my thoughts. I don't let them, I will never let them get to you. Don't worry, I'll never let them touch you. I'll never sell you out.

Tonight I will be with you, entwined. Your smile will light one thousand jungles on fire. We will hover above the war torn filth machine that this city is. In my thoughts I am invincible. When we touch, we are all things.

The sun is setting, the dirty air is clawing at my lungs. 1000 razored eyes try to rip me to shreds as I hurry along. I hear their tiny words as I pass. "Look, he moves like a rat!" I am almost to my hole. I will be with you soon. For now, this miserable thought will have to do. I have so much to tell you. It will take time and it will be fractured like me. I know you understand me.

I'm walking on a bridge. My back is to the sun, my face is to the abyss. Will you come with me? Demon sun burning my back with red eyes. My pupils being sucked out by the vacant spaces in their faces. We are the only ones left. Don't let them scar you with their weakness. They will cripple you with their lives, they will make you want to die just to get away from them. They don't know how dangerous they are, they are immune to their own poison. That's the way they keep doing it to each other life after life.

Sometimes I feel like glass, if I breathe too hard I will implode. I can feel the ground glass in my guts. I'm an alien and I don't

remember the last time a human made me feel anything at all.
Sometimes I feel frozen like a piece of iron. Like a factory that's
been shut down. Right now I am frozen. My thoughts are frozen
fingers, like a spider made of ice. In your eyes I see a flame, it
draws me to you. You are everything to me.

I sing songs to you. I live in front of strangers. They freeze me
out, they empty me. I feel like an old warehouse. Do you want
me?
Tonight
You and I walk together in the Fall air
Street lamps throw down shadowed light
The leaves under our feet
Imagine that, for once not alone
I can close my eyes and see it
I can breathe in and smell the wood burning fire
Miles away from this hotel room
The fake air that claws my throat
Grey walls that reduce my eyes
To instruments of torture
Tonight, I am the king of self infliction
You and me on this autumn night
I can't talk to them
You should hear my words kill themselves
I cripple myself with them
The closer I get, the farther away I know I am
Tonight my heart incinerates my guts. My eyes freeze and burn
in their sockets. Have you ever fallen into yourself and gotten
lost? I'm so far from them, yet at times I wish for them. I wish I
could understand them and deal with them without all the pain
and bitterness that comes with contact. At times I wish for them
to touch me. Strangers pass by me in this wounded leaking night.

They burn me, vile weaklings. I hide my face in my hands
when they pass knowing my gaze would turn them to stone. They

can't stop my eyes from their righteous penetration. They see too much. I want to smash my head like a glass melon, stick pins into my eyes and let it all pour onto the floor. There must be kindness in blindness because there is none in this present clarity.

EXHAUSTION BLUES

Exhaustion, I thought I would check in with you:

Right now it's autumn, I'm in Germany. Spring and summer make me think in the present, autumn and winter paralyze me. Autumn makes me remember, forces me into mental rewind.

Today we were in the van driving thru a small village and I caught the smell of a wood burning fire. It sent me, I inhaled again but it was gone. Made me think of when I was in 4th grade, I delivered papers for the Washington Star. In the autumn the sun would set early and it would be dark by the time I would finish the route. I could smell the wood burning fires all over, every block. Another thought comes in to interrupt: A few months ago I was at the New Music Seminar. That bullshit wheel they run every year so the labels can all go and tell each other how great they are. This time around we played at the seminar. It was a good gig as far as gigs go. It was a drag having to be around all these people from nowhere peddling their music. I was put on the artist panel to answer questions from the audience. There were some interesting people on the panel. I sat next to Hank Ballard, he was a trip. I talked to Leonard Cohen, he was cool. That little shit from the Police was there. Lemmy was on the panel, he was a drunk disappointment, pathetic. So anyway, we're all lined up behind this long table and the mediator is a shithead. He's asking all the panelists a bunch of stupid shit, trying to piss them off. He asked Leonard Cohen what it was like to fuck Nico in the Chelsea Hotel, stupid ass shit like that. Some bright penny sent a question up to the front for me to answer. Something like "Having grown up serving designer ice cream to fellow rich kids in a nice neighborhood, how can you reconcile what you do now?" What the fuck kind of question is that? It's the kind of thing you ask when you want to get smacked. That's what should have happened. It would have been great if the guy had come up front and asked the question and then I climbed down from the stage and punched him once and walk back to my seat. That would have been high class entertainment as well as an art statement. Nietzsche called them "the tiny masters of today," little shitheels. They never get what they need so bad. So anyway, I would throw papers until past dark and then I would stay out as long as I could with out freezing my ass off. I did all I could to stay out of the house, I didn't want to be in there if I could help it. I knew that my mother would be home and I wanted to stay away from her as much as possible. It was alright though, I would hang out and walk the streets passing the time. I liked being out on the streets, it's where I felt best. Home was always painful when she was there. On the streets I could be alone to be with my own thoughts. Looking back on it now it was good that it went down that way. I learned to be self reliant at an early age.

The autumn always makes me think of women, something about the cold air that brings life to a woman's face. Perhaps it's just that I'm lonely at that point in the year, always rocking out in some shithole. But you know, it's a false loneliness because for the life of me, I can't think of a single woman that I would want to be with. I like the ones in my imagination the best. The ones that I think up in the van as the miles fly by. They are the women that I tell myself about after shows when I am feeling empty and alone. The women that fill the lie, that fill the void for awhile until I can get onto other thoughts. Sometimes it's hard not to get lost in yourself on these tours. All these people in your face, nothing like it to make you know that you're totally alone. The isolation is vivid, and then there's you, Exhaustion. You always come in near the end of a tour to remind me that I'm not 20 anymore.

Sometimes I think I'm from another planet. I bet a lot of people feel that way too. Like no one will know them and that they'll never fit into this screaming horrific bullshit festival. They try to hold onto something and somehow it falls out of their grasp, or even worse, it sits just out of reach. You can get to feeling displaced, feeling noplaced. I have grown accustomed to feeling alien everywhere I go, it's no big deal. I remember when I used to get off work. I would go eat in the same hamburger place every night. People would always be staring at me, looking at my bald head. At first it used to trip me out and get me mad, but after awhile I could be in a room full of people staring and I wouldn't even care. You get a strange distance from people that you never get back all the way, no matter what happens. Once you have been on the outside, a part of you will always be out there. It's a good thing too. If you let them, they'll waste your time and make you sick until there's nothing left of you. Every time they push you out, you get more of yourself in return. I figure it's a good deal, seeing how many people have no clue to who they are. Waiting all night by the phone hoping that someone will call. Going out with people they don't care about or don't even like because they can't stand the thought of being alone. Because the thought of being alone tells them that they're failures, that people that are alone are always lonely and miserable. I hear so many stories about people having to lie all night because they were out with someone they didn't like and had to keep up some kind of appearance. That's the shit that gives you nervous breakdowns and cancer. All this shit makes me feel the same way every time. People for the most part are a waste of time. The more time you get to yourself the better.

When I had wheels I used to spend more time in my car than in my apartment. I had a shitty tape deck in there and I would drive around just to hear the music. There was this Dunkin' Donuts I used to go to and hang out by myself. Every moment spent away from my boss, from people I knew, every moment I spent making my own world, I felt better. I would hang out in this place and drink coffee and listen to the locals talk a bunch of shit and try to untangle the last four years out of my brain. I didn't know what to do with all the hatred that I had inside. I tried to write but it didn't work. A good healthy level of hate is always good to have on hand at all times. There's nothing wrong with it. Hate gets you thru times where love just confuses and entraps. Hate is so final and pure, love is always many headed and dangerous. I know hate is good because I see how many people don't know how to deal with it. They don't see it for the energy force it can be. When it rises in them, they run headlong into a stranger that lives inside. They don't know themselves and it tears them up when they need themselves the most. They don't have themselves to go to, they were always too busy burning the wax trying to look good for someone else. Trying to be someone's something. What a sellout.

There's certain music that only works for me in the autumn. Sitting in this cold ass club makes me want to hear Lou Reed. When I came thru here with the Flag in 1983, it was February. It was cold as shit, we played this Velvet Underground tape as we limped from show to show. Ever since then, it's always been Lou in the autumn and winter. His album "Street Hassle" got me thru many cold weather blues, still does.

I can't remember an autumn in the last several years when I wasn't in a van driving down some grey vacant highway. Cold weather makes me think clearer and makes me more withdrawn than usual. I'm not close to people, I am close to myself. I spend a lot of time inside. Where else can you go when everything pushes you to every edge in the joint. You have to make your head your home. It's the only way to withstand places like the one that I'm in tonight. If you can't pull into yourself, you're finished. The road will crush you. Nothing like Europe for exercises in isolation, that's why I like it here. Last night was good, after the show was over I sat behind the PA and listened to music. No one could see me so I could hang out without having to talk to anyone. After shows people can really bring me down. They ask questions that I can't understand. They want to talk about what they just saw. The last thing that I want to think about is playing live. If you do it then you know not to talk about it. Sometimes when they ask questions, I can tell by what they want to know that the distance between me and them is so far. It's really depressing, I see that I really am all alone out there. It was good to just be able to listen to music and not have to see or talk to anyone. I don't even want to talk to the guys in the band after playing. I just want to sit and try to pick up the pieces as best I can. There's a great feeling when you're totally resolved. When you make the jump from being lonely to being only. When you're so totally alone and absolute, when you are the number one. This is a great moment. Finally you know something, it's all yours. When I have put myself thru the human test and come thru it still being able to say my name and knowing that there's nothing else for me and no one for me. I become stronger. My will power grows. I push my pain threshold out farther. I'm able to take more, I'm able to learn more.

I have made myself an enemy of praise and adulation. Let me explain the reason for this. Praise is dangerous, it can go from a little to too much in a few words. Sure it's nice to know that someone likes what you do. You can see what it does to the rockstar types that believe the reviews and all the things that everyone says. To take it all the way, you must turn a deaf ear to praise, move and keep moving. The last thing I want to hear is that someone likes what I do. When someone starts in with it I try to change the subject. I know that I'm probably more extreme than most in this respect but I have found that praise fucks me up. I like it best having little or no interaction with people at all, that's not to say that I don't like the people that come to the road house to see the show. I feel a great responsibility to these strangers.

They take time out of their lives to check out what I'm doing, I'm honored but I don't want to hear the rub. I am systematically destroying myself piece by piece and I don't need to be complimented on it.

You have to be careful because it all can turn on you. I find myself in bad situations where I ask myself if I should never talk to anyone again. I just want to get on with the work, the rest doesn't matter. Seeing someone that you haven't seen for years, and they tell you what your problems are and that you're nothing but an asshole anyway. You're in that magazine, who do you think you are. And I think to myself about the long drives and all the bullshit that anyone on the road has to put up with. I pull back from that thought and look at a guy my age with a beer gut and an attitude giving me shit. It's sad when someone you know becomes someone you knew, that's the bottom line. It makes me very hard and wary around people. If I'm not careful I'll slip into ugly ruts of cynical bullshit. I don't want to be like that. Exhaustion, you're a disease.

Best not to mix the past with the present. The present paints the past with gold, the past paints the present with lead. When I run backwards I feel the desperation rise. Best for me to hurtle headlong into the present. Never look back. Maybe catch on fire if I do it right.

That's all there is. The Right Now. If we don't plant ourselves in the front row of the present, I predict that if any of us reach old age, we'll be sitting on the front porch thinking "Damn, shoulda burned all the temples, screamed and danced and dragged life thru the coals." I align myself with life's brutal headlong lunge towards Death. I am in motion at all times. Waging war with you, Exhaustion. Winning some and losing some.

BLACK COFFEE BLUES

1.27.89 Brisbane Australia
Broken roach wings on the floor
You get your wings in places like this
You earn your roach wings
They keep you up
Not suspended
But eye to eye with an understanding
An understanding that keeps your mouth clamped shut
When you're with your woman
When she asks you what's the matter
In the painful silence you can hear the roach wings fluttering
In this room on the floor by my right foot
Dead belly up legs folded
Roach wings won't get you far but they'll get you here
This circuit tour circle wheel
Rolling after its own tail
Your life becomes a series of events
A page on a calendar
A wind up a pitch and a roar
A head full of traffic jammed broken glass memories

3.4.89 Vienna Austria 7:59 AM: It rarely gets better than this. I'm
in the breakfast room of this old hotel. The grey light of the
Austrian morning puts a soft cast on the empty tables that
surround me. Across from where I'm sitting is a long table of
food: eggs, cheese, bread, rolls, butter, jam, milk, orange juice,
muesli, and a large pot full of black coffee. I am halfway thru the
first cup, awesome. There are slight beads of sweat developing on
my brow.

I've stayed in this hotel before in 1987. The band was playing

10 weeks of shows across Europe. The table we sat at is to my left. What a great, mighty morning it was. We ate so much food that I think they were going to throw us out if we so much as even looked at the food table again. It was fantastic, an exercise in overeating, "Sport Eating" we used to call it in Black Flag. After we had eaten too much food, we made sandwiches for the road, put them in our pockets and exited.

I have finished the first cup. I ask the friendly young woman if I can have some more coffee. Her reply endears her to me until checkout time. "Yes, of course." she says, she understands. The second cup has arrived.

This hotel is across the road from the train station. In '87 I walked the streets here on a night off. I went into the station and watched an amputee try to sleep on a bench, he was rousted and expelled. I watched the whores work the Blvd in their thigh-high white plastic boots. Last night as I was getting back from the club, I thought about taking a walk down to where I saw this beautiful blond whore hold up the side of a building. She was a hot icy sex merchant machine. Last night I thought about her as I stared into the darkness of my room. I wondered where she was, maybe still out on the Blvd, maybe dead. Was she still as pretty as I remembered? Is anyone? How memories lie to us. How time coats the ordinary with gold, how it breaks the heart to go back and attempt to re-live them. How crushed we are when we discover that the gold was merely gold plate thinly coated over lead, chalk and peeling paint.

She comes forward, a pot in each hand. "Would you like another cup of coffee?" she asks. "Yes, please." I reply, thru clenched teeth, trying to pull my right hand from my leg, which is gripping it so hard, I might be cutting off the circulation. She pours it. There it sits, black and ominous, a slight oil slick at the top. I drink, smooth, like Death.

Today I go to Budapest, Hungary where the idea of coffee is

but a joke. Hard to find and when you score, it usually tastes like instant that has been stored and aged in the bladder of a goat. I see why they drink so much booze.

As I drink, I think of her, the beautiful whore. Since I saw her, she has probably sucked ten kilometers of cock, gained an incredible insight into the frailties and insecurities of the average male, seen enough to know that she's seen too much, and knows enough to know that sometimes it's better not to know it all. You brave, beautiful sex beast. This third cup is for you.
Excuse me, I must be on my way.

3.6.89 Linz Austria: Staring at cup #3, not so hot. Not half as hot as the waitresses in this place, same girls as last time. They act the same way too, cold and distant. Tonight feels empty. Spent the day driving thru the countryside of Hungary and Austria. I don't know, something in this place is pulling me down. The waitress is wearing perfume, it smells like something wonderful. Good thing the coffee is here to blast me thru. Sometimes you hit these situations where all you can do is endure, take it minute by minute. It's good though, to be in this room full of voices and not be able to understand a word of what anyone is saying. I like this lean feeling that moves relentlessly thru me. Sometimes I feel like a perfect stranger, like I was born to be forever isolated from them. Do you know what I'm talking about? Totally alien. Heavy coffee blues #3 is hanging in there, staring up at me. People all around me talking. I'm on another planet. I don't feel lonely, just anxious and confused. People staring, I hear my name start to pop up in their conversation. Forces my eyes to the paper, to the coffee, the oily black eye of Truth!

For the life of me I can't figure out the women here. Are they made of wood or ice or a combination of both. I observe them. I don't talk to them unless one of them asks me a direct question, otherwise I have nothing to say to them. Who is them? Them are them. Them are everywhere. I don't understand them. I used to think I did but now I see that I was wrong. I was fooling myself. All the hours I spent fooling myself. Everybody fools themselves sometime. The better of us spend less of their waking hours doing this I think. There is, however, a lot to be said for those who are good at being foolish, they get all the headlines.

3.7.89 Linz Austria
Alone in a room
Music playing on the tape deck
Staring at the floor
Single bulb stares down
Waiting for sleep
Waiting for the brain to pause
Hours ago in another room
Talking in front of a bunch of people
Now I'm here
No one knows
So what
I can stack hundreds of nights like this
Like bricks
Build it higher and higher
It's what happens anyway
So what
It takes no guts to do that
I have found it takes a lot of strength
To endure myself
It gets harder all the time
I don't know
If I'm getting smarter and stronger
Or better at fooling myself

3.8.89 Dortmund Germany: Do I have a mind left? How many

cups has it been? Why am I doing this to myself? I staggered into the breakfast room half an hour ago, half a day ago. Half an hour, half a day? Awhile ago the coffee lady gave me some shit because I poured the coffee myself and didn't let her do it. All I could was smile, look away, and try to repress the urge to rip her throat out. The rain is falling in Dortmund. It rained last time I was here.

Something Selby said to me yesterday about romance made me start thinking. Right now the coffee is on, the black blood of the almighty coffee god is surging thru me. I can do nothing but give myself to the storm.

Romance, shit. There's this girl I used to see in LA, she was always giving me shit about my total lack of romantic attitude. One time I told her that love and romance had "been beaten out of me." Sure it was one of the stupidest things I have ever said in my life but I thought it would have great impact on her, a great foil for one of my typically male hang-ups. She never let me forget that one. She would say shit like, "Why don't you send me flowers sometime. Oh wait that's romantic. I forgot, it's been beaten out of you. So sorry." Well it's 1989, I'm 28 years old and sex is not a new experience for me. At this point it's bio-mekanikal. Perhaps I blew it somewhere along the line.

I had a brief, fleeting brush with romance a couple of years ago. I had dreams about her, I wrote things about her, to her. I didn't even know her name. She was working at this place that I used to go into a lot. At that point she was perfect, she could do no wrong. It was great, a total non-reality. ROMANCE. Eventually I got together with her and for a short while it was great. I went on tour somewhere. Wrote her all the time, called her twice from thousands of miles away. Her response was always the same. It was like I was calling her from right down the street. She couldn't care less. When I got home she had written me a letter. It said that she didn't want to be with me anymore. I found more interest in working hard than following the whims of non-business related or non-musical relationships.

The next song I wrote was about the distance I felt when I thought about that girl. The song centered around the lines "the closer I get, the farther away I feel." I was thinking that all the time I was with her. I worked hard to put that out of my mind. Romance passes the time.

Selby said that he wanted some romance in his life. He said he enjoyed sending flowers to and cards to someone. There's nothing wrong with that I guess, besides that's Selby talking and he is the man. There's this girl I know, she sends me flowers and cards and all kinds of shit. Of course I throw them out immediately and think of all the things I could've done with the money she spent on all that garbage. After we fuck, she disappears into the bathroom. Minutes later she reappears with a damp washcloth and wipes my cock off. Isn't that nice. The Hallmark greeting card company should make a card for that one, with a nice one liner "You're so beautiful when you're wiping the juice off my spent cock."

Maybe I have become burned out. A typical male, a mean assed slothful fucker, a real American beauty. It's a form of blindness, vaseline on the lense, no problem. I know you're laughing now, thinking that I am such a dick...fine. I am the last man, the unromantic one, the one who sees it all as a big-ass biology party. Well ok. Maybe someday I'll snap out of it, but for right now...make mine hot and black, fill it to the top and don't talk.

3.10.89 Berlin Germany: What goes best with a cup of coffee? Another cup. This morning's pot has its own burner, it sits faithfully to my left. A few hours from now I'll be on the road to Koln, Germany.

Today's sky is grey. I am alone in the breakfast room of a large hotel. I ate with Selby this morning. We have been doing this the last few days. He is such a great man, it's an honor to be on the road with him. To be around him all the time, to see him work every night. It means a lot to me. Everything.

Ah yes we drink the coffee and we feel the isolation settle in. Picture yourself at the table staring absently at a crack in its surface. Your eyes a vacant lot for all the garbage and all that is lost and thrown away. All the people you knew, past experiences, ten lifetimes of grey skies, a planet of rainstorms fill you. You are totally alone with yourself. You take a long walk thru yourself without moving. You don't remember when it was when you sat down. Time doesn't exist for a little while. The isolation, the isolation that we all feel. Sometimes it's so clearly defined that it becomes another entity altogether. It sits across from you and shares the empty space of shattered time. Freedom can be a vacant lot. It fills you with nothing and then leaves you to figure it out. Isolation keeps me together. All the hours spent in the van staring at the passing road. I wrap myself around myself. Isolated parts starving for isolated parts that are starving. We can only get so close. In this truth there is a rough, lean beauty. A straight line. Even when together we are apart. I think that there are moments, instances of power, of time outside of time. Moments that are truly larger than life.

At first I had problems with the isolation. I didn't understand it as truth. I fought it within myself and I tore myself up inside. Once I saw and understood the isolation, new doors immediately opened for me.

The end of the line defines the line. At the end of the line, there you are alone. Life was a flash, a handshake in the dark. In the lonely room packed with people: there they are, there you are. Truth screaming in your face. Sometimes the night is a sharp punch in the guts.

3.20.89 Amsterdam Holland: Tonight is crawling by like a well fed roach. Alone in my hotel room. Fucking cheap town Amsterdam is. Hash dealing freaks staggering. Their sales pitches mixed with rattling coughs. One guy followed me into a bank. I contemplated a shot to the head but you can't be doing that shit in a public place. You don't want to get into shit with pigs in a place like this. That would be something though, to dump a Dutch cop. The hotel here serves up the awesome coffee. I'm seeing the light, I am feeling the great weight. I have been coming to this hotel since November 1985. I was speaking at the One World Poetry Festival. A lot of cool people were there. Jefferey Lee Pierce, LKJ, Z'ev, they were so great. One morning I came into the lobby and there was Mufti from Einsturzende Neubauten asleep on the floor, waiting for a room to be opened for him.

Tonight is a night off, it's getting on near midnight. The moon is full and shining down on the canal in front of the hotel. Good to be alone. Sometimes I wish the night would last forever. Daylight brings the static human confusion overload. Have been having a hard time keeping from caving in on myself. I feel so hollow. I don't want to be with someone else. It's just another nowhere, another gesture, a lie. Sometimes life is such an old joke. Another night in some hotel room in some city in some country somewhere. I chainsmoke nights like these. Small lit cubes these rooms. The nights are the stitches that hold me together. All the faces have fallen away, I see no one in this dream. Isaac Hayes on the tape deck singing "Walk On By." I used to play that when I would be feeling lonely. Now when I play it, I hear it differently. It's not as good. Fuck this. I have to get out of this room and get some air.

3.21.89 Amsterdam Holland: Walking from your hotel to the city center without getting hit by a car, a bike, or a street car is something of a triumph. I wonder how many tourists have been done in by the flying Dutchmen of old Amsterdam.

I bet the residents of Amsterdam have a love/hate relationship with tourists. They love the money that they bring into the town and they hate their guts just as much.

This morning while on my way to a record store I heard a group of young men speaking English. They had surrounded a large group of pigeons and were kicking them to death. One said "Look at them there eagles!" Another said "I wish I had my .22, I would blow them all away!" Americans in Europe, look out.

Tourists buying blocks of dried dogshit thinking it's hash. Running back to their hotel rooms and smoking it up, thinking that this city is so cool to be able to buy this good shit right there in the street. Some Dutch guy with a pocket full of guilders laughing his ass off, thanking the USA. He sees a dog taking a shit at an intersection and says in his best Southern Californian accent "Hash dude, awesome!"

The Dutch have mastered the dead-pan reply. That's the one where they make you feel like an incredible asshole. No matter what you ask, you will be answered as if someone is reading to you from a book on Russian history. The more energy you put into a question or a greeting, the more you will be halted by slow measured speech which often contains better grammar than you will ever possess. If you make a joke, the Dutchman will retreat ten big steps down the hallway of ultra-infinite cool.

Back to the subject of the homicidal tendencies of the Dutch roadways. One thing I've noticed about the drivers. They have their eyes keenly and intensely focused on everything except what is directly in front of them. Today I heard a lot of beeping resulting in bellows and shouts in French, German, English and Spanish, none in Dutch. Yup, tourists all. Be careful carefree travelers. It would be such a shame to send you home to Carbondale, Illinois in an American Express Euro-Fun body bag.

3.22.89 Nijamagen Holland: Powering some grade B coffee in a graffiti covered backstage room here in Nijmagen Holland. Cold inside, raining and dark outside. This place reminds me of this place I played in Australia a few months ago. There was this dressing room with all these dead cockroaches on the floor, their little wings scattered all over. Tonight the brittle roach wings flap in my ear, flying low. Writing blues songs effortlessly. On the other side of this wall, the club is showing a live video of Black Flag. I hear the song Slip It In pound thru the wall. Life pushes you around gets you all caught up. It confuses and trips you. Nights like these, passing the time, waiting to get on stage and bleed in front of strangers. That's what I do.

When I go on tours outside of the USA, the term "Back to the World" keeps coming up in my thoughts. When I come off a tour and have to deal with people that I haven't talked to in months, it becomes clear that I have nothing in common with them at all. It's as if I have stepped off a spaceship and the world outside of the tour is some alien planet. All I can do is be as cool as possible for as long as possible and get away as quickly as I can. I have nothing to do with them and the world they live in. The only place to go is back on tour, back to rooms like these. Here is better, just getting on with it. What else is there, nothing. Not for me at least.

APRIL 1989 New York City
The subway from Brooklyn was filthy this morning
Been heading north on Amtrak
The pretty girl got out hours ago
Near Canada now
I can see the bottoms of the streams
Still it can't wash the ghettos from my mind
The view ravages my thoughts
Another fist into my brain
Sometimes it all feels like fists
And sometimes I feel like a Deathtrip rider, scorched

Laughing at these people when they say they're burning in hell
All romance turns low speed porno
Last night I was in Hoboken NJ
Kicking a show out of my system
I listened to this poet
Bloated and fucked up
Reading shit he wrote in 1971
What happens to these people?
Motherfucker should have changed his last name to Heck
Been out on this one almost 9 weeks
That is my reality
Swinging on a hinge
Almost to Canada
It's not over until you're dead
Talked to a reporter from Melody Maker this morning
What did I do that for
There's no one farther away from reality than a critic
They have the great flawed weapon
The question for which there is no answer
If he had gotten in the van for the last 8 years
He wouldn't have to ask
Robert Johnson knew
Sting doesn't know
Edie Brickell never will
All the great story tellers keep their mouths shut
Long train ride
Hard to keep up morale and sense of purpose
Some times I see pointlessness all too clearly

April 1989 Montreal Canada: I can't find her. I keep looking. I'm tired of feeling above it all. I want to be taught a lesson. I want to know if my heart can be broken. Is it hard as iron or am I a gutless wonder. I want to meet a woman that will make me stop and listen to what she has to say. I want a woman that will make my jaw drop in awe. A woman that has little time for me. One that does not throw herself at me. One who has self respect, who has a sense of herself. Where is she. I wish she was here right now. I'm in a hotel that also serves as a place for whores to take their trade. When I came in I saw this young man being led in by a whore, he looked a bit scared. The man at the desk looked at the young man like he was another sucker. What a fucked up room this is. Have a long way to before this thing is over. Should try to get some sleep. There's a woman screaming in the room next to mine.

10.10.89 Toronto Canada: After shows I sit on the floor sweating. Sometimes steam comes off me. People come up and talk to me, I'm not much good at this point. All I can do is pretend to hear what they're saying to me. The last thing I want to do is talk. I have nothing to say to anyone. I figure I said it already. The people who want to talk to me are usually friendly and really cool. Hell they came to the show and they thought enough of what was done to come back and talk about it. I can respect that. Sometimes there's too many people, like last night. It's easy to lose your temper. After playing hard you might want a minute to rest. I sit still, arms wrapped around myself. There is no time when I feel more like the total embodiment of all that I do this for. To be total and to embody the number 1. At this time I see clearly, all things have been stripped away. My body is full of pain and it feels good. It's the reward for having reached beyond myself. I learn the lesson. I stare perspective in the face, it stares back. We lock in total agreement. Sometimes after a show I can barely get up to change, but I know that I'm stronger than I was a few hours before.

11.4.89 Leeds UK: Walking the wet streets in Leeds. Goth rockers, dipped in black leather. Sad, sexless, miserable. They walk bandy-legged across the park. This city has been slapped in the face with coat of grey poison.

Last night a kid came up to me and told me that he'll have to walk 25 miles to get home because his ride left him behind. He said he didn't mind and told me to keep coming back.

Walked for hours, got a haircut. Lied to the lady when she asked me about the tattoos. Had tea in this shopping mall. Old women, fat legs and folded faces. Fried food diet for five decades, lard in the blood, silt at the bottom of the brain. Chew the water and don't breathe the air.

Walked by Chris' old house, 52 Harold Mount. The place where we wrote all the stuff for Hot Animal Machine in October 1987. This time there was a girl sitting in the kitchen where I used to sit at six in the morning, desperately trying to write songs.

Damn these days off. Give me work so I don't have to constantly consume myself. I turn corners, I keep seeing myself mirrored in the bricks. This city fills me with an alien strain of stagnating, suffocating sadness and regret. A pinpoint on the map, mental quicksand. Trudge thru the park, cold wind mixed with tiny rain. Like getting coughed on by a corpse. Sure I'm good, good at fooling myself so I can sidestep despair with the grace of matador. I can wear a weary smile and carry it off quite well. Like all human insulation, it's cowardly and sometimes downright mandatory to get thru some of the shit that gets thrown your way. To be able to pull away from a night that's reminding you of all the things that trip you up. I know you know what I mean.

11.6.89 Brighton UK: Brighton Beach full of people-like organisms. Sitting in a food shop waiting for the tea and veggie burger atomic greaseball dinner to hit the table. Cold outside, Clash tape playing over the sound system, tape is full of dropouts. Sounds like old Joe is going thru some guitar effect. The others ran into

Paul Simonon the other night in some curry place near our hotel in London. The PA in the club we're playing tonight is a toy, the stage is tiny and the backstage area is small and cold. Welcome to England. It could be worse. I could have to stay here another day. With any luck I'll be out of the UK soon. It's funny, every time I come here I swear that I will never play here again and then we get the offer to play and I always say yes. What the fuck, a gig is a gig.

11.14.89 ? Germany: Walked the streets today. Day off, day off from what? Posters for Last Exit to Brooklyn are up, they look great, way to go Cubby. Sat in a cafe tonight, breathed in second hand smoke. Listened to the talk I didn't understand. I wrote a song called Loneliness is a Crushing Wheel. Now I'm in a hotel room alone. Roy Orbison burning cold blue on the tape deck. Tried to write a postcard to someone, gave up after three lines, nothing to say. I hope I don't dream tonight. Sometimes you can get so far inside yourself that you don't know who you are. I try to shake it off by walking. The sound of my feet and the sound of the cars passing brings me back to life. In these rooms it all closes in on you. Lonely as hell, makes you swallow all the good and the bad at once. I face myself, endlessly analyze, rip apart and mutate. No dreams please.

11.16.89 Geneva Switzerland: The DJ is playing Bad Brains over the PA. The song "At The Movies" comes on. I remember when I sat in Paul Cleary's car and Darryl played me a demo version, that was 1980 I think. The song "I" rolls by and I remember watching them work on that in Nathan's basement. What does one do with one's past? When I sit in the van for hours at a time I walk backwards thru myself and think about the things that have happened. A word that I despise comes into my thoughts, that word is "regret." I hate that one. Regret is an ugly and destructive luxury. It must be avoided at all costs. Today I thought about all the years on the road with Black Flag. The road has a way of turning me on myself. The road keeps coming back in my face. Confusion, comparison, they trip me. I find it hard to deal with my past. Sometimes I feel like locking myself away so I won't have to see faces and places that remind me of faces and places. The shit plagues me, like playing some place for the 5th time. On this tour, I played a place in Amsterdam where I turned 22 onstage. Sometimes it's hard to convince yourself that you're not an idiot, sometimes you can't do it.

11.20.89 Frankfurt Germany: Bitterness. When everything seems like it wants to see you die. You bump your head on self doubt. Despair runs circles around you flashing its teeth. You recoil with bitterness, you feel dizzy and sick. You feel the sickness of the entire world coursing thru your body. You become filled with pure hatred for all that is. You find all things poisonous. You reel like an ocean of sickness. What brings on this bitterness?

I find much bitterness in myself. My desire for great heights brings me crashing down to the terra firma of reality. Expectations I had for myself, thinking that bullshit was real, expecting more out of people. Our shortcomings leave me splintered and alienated. Entertaining my archenemy, hope. Judging others, making them adhere to my strict value system so that I can feel unthreatened by them instead of letting them be themselves. These things have sent me staggering into the darkness, lungs full of bitterness.

The desire to possess, the will to lust. These things have brought me countless nights of bitterness. Example: I am sitting in a club waiting to play. A beautiful woman walks into the place, her beauty intoxicates me. She walks by me, the same beauty that intoxicated me moments before now infuriates me. I have made her beauty my problem. Beauty can fill one with loathing. How convenient to put your need on someone else's shoulders. The smell of a woman's perfume is enough to ruin an otherwise perfect day. It's also easy to hate someone for their virtue or talent because it makes you feel small, bitter to the core.

Bitterness is the core joy of self pity. Bitterness reflects the result of when expectation meets reality. You wallow in the self inspired swamp of your misery. A great way to meet yourself!

Bitterness due to overload, too much. Perspective and reason can become blurred or lost altogether. Bitterness from fatigue. On tour I get asked the same questions every night. I get tired of answering the same thing. Like if you had to say hello to every person that passed you, you would get tired of the word and tired of people. You might even start hating their guts for no reason. You could start hating people for their good intentions, that's when you need a definite "attitude adjustment."

It's easy to become so full of shit that you become deaf, dumb and blind to common sense and good reason. I am constantly working to rid myself of the bullshit. I win some and lose some, but I keep working all the same. The coffee in this place is hell and we don't go on until 1:30 in the morning.

11.28.89 Zagreb Yugoslavia: It's almost dark now. I was told that it was a holiday today. All the stores are closed. Few people on the streets. Mostly soldiers walking in small groups, their long green coats flapping in the wind. Zagreb looks strange to me. A block of buildings, ancient, ready to fall over faces a row of buildings all shining glass and neon. The streets look tired, looted. Spray paint scars the fronts of the older buildings, this place looks like a frozen ghost town.

Exhaustion was what I wanted to get to. 36 shows down, 10 more to go. Exhaustion has found me. Every morning I wake up tired. I keep myself to myself during the day, time usually spent in the van watching the scenery pass by the window. I don't want to talk and the rest leave me alone to my thoughts. I keep my energy for the show that night. The only thing that makes all of this worth it is the chance to play at night. The music is the reward for feeling like you have carried someone's luggage up 5 miles of stairs.

12.16.89 Los Angeles CA: Pathetic: In 1987 there was this woman I was spending some time with. It was the first time in a long time that I had been into someone and it felt great. I was out on this tour and she called me and asked if she could come visit for a day or so. I thought it would be great. I was wrong. She flew out to the city where we were. I hardly saw her most of the day because of soundcheck, interviews and then stretching before hitting stage. After the show, she and I get this hotel room. We're in there and all I can do is stare at the wall. I was tired from playing and my mind was on the road. I tried to find words to tell her that I was burnt. I didn't pull it off. She got pissed off. Me with my silence and my limp dick. The next day she told me to fuck off and she left. After the show that night, I was in the parking lot looking at these pictures of her that I had. I started to cry. I was so mad at myself. I looked saw all these people gathered in a semi circle staring at me. I didn't hear them come up. I must have looked pretty stupid. What the fuck was I supposed to do. I walked thru them and tore the pics up and threw them into a dumpster. I walked back to the van and there was this guy from the local newspaper wanting to take pictures of the band. Must have looked like I was stoned, with the red eyes and everything. I got over it after awhile. Since then I haven't let anyone get that close to me.

12.20.89 Los Angeles CA:
Don't hold onto time
It moves with or without you

It's like trying to hold onto a passing train
Don't hold onto people
All you do is hurt yourself
I come back from a tour with a dull roar in my ears. In my mind
I play back the last show. How I walked off the stage, never telling
the audience that it was the last show on the tour. It's none of their
business. I remember walking up the stairs to the dressing room.
While I walk I remember the ends of other tours over the last 9
years. I enter the dressing room. There's no one there but me. I
drink from a bottle of water, my sweat is turning to ammonia. I
can smell it, I stink. Two girls come in and try to talk to me. I tell
them to get out. Two days later I'm back in my room, jet lagged
from the Frankfurt to LA flight. I feel like talking to someone. I
feel a vacancy. I don't know what to do with the night when it's
gig time. After 50 shows in 60 days it's all I know how to do. I'm
lonely for the tour. I miss the van and the road and the smell of
the gasoline. I look at the floor and I feel like shit. Finally I come
to my senses and let it go. When I let it go, it lets me go. When
it's over, it's over.
Let it go or it turns on you
Don't attach
Don't hold onto anyone's anything
Throw out memories
Pull them out like bad teeth
Don't attach
What was, was
It's not easy to face

2.12.90 San Francisco CA:
Oh yea: We got to get that one on tape. We have to make a
document out of that thought. A monument out of that tomb. A
hero out of that corpse. A lifestyle out of that criminal. Yea we got
to get the awesome picture of that, quick, get the light just right,

damn, we blew it, we had it right there and we let it go...

Oh no: Sitting on the front porch, a whole mess of time on our hands. So much time that we had to get up at the crack of dawn to start plowing thru it. So much of this time stuff did we possess that we had to stay up till near 4:00 in the morning on foot, skateboards and bikes trying to chew our way thru it. Steaming down endless cracked sidewalks and pitted streets. The median stripes radiating Death and abundance under the relentless inspection of the crime lights that hovered above at iron tree stamina straightness. We were hypnotized by the neon, rust and the raw fact that we were alive right then, righteously so. We were as alive as the power lines crackling. Alive like the dictionary's definition of the word explosion. We were blind and full of shit but we were alive. Throwing off ballast, insults, clumsy threats, promises and other taunts at Death.

Oh well: Here I am. Looking down, looking back, looking for broken pieces to put together. Making out like a desperate detective trying to find out where it went. Looking high and low for clues. All the while, time is doubled over with laughter. "LOOKING FOR ME?" Now I know. All time happens right now. The finger is pointed at me. There is only one direction.

2.20.90 3:36 AM Los Angeles CA: Can't sleep. Got my mind on my mind. I think I think too much. Been thinking about my friend the hotel room. I feel more at home in those than I do here.

Sure would be good to get back out to Europe. Been thinking about it ever since I got back here. So great to be in a room full of people and not have to know what they're talking about.

Tonight I fill the room with thoughts. I push out the unmoving air and replace it with my thoughts. Shifting rain, heat lightning, red neon shining on a wet sidewalk. Rain falling on the roof at 3 am.

5.21.90 Bondi Beach Australia:
Light bulb
You are my company tonight
You make me see that this room is hell
I know you saw that roach crawl up my leg
You made it look like a stumbling gem
As it made its escape across the carpet
Just between you and me
I don't think anyone understands anyone else
It's past 3 am
I'm hungry and everything's closed
I get caught in Time's lockdown
Hey light bulb I was thinking
You never get to use yourself
You have a great gift
I wish I could turn myself off and on
Like I can do to you

9.3.90 Germany:
Somewhere in Germany near the Austrian border
3:37 AM cold and raining
People huddled in the doorway of the WC
The attendant bored tired and smoking
I feel good
I haven't slept and I can smell myself
I am hours away from my destination
My eyes ache, I feel great
I mean it
The smell of diesel and tobacco smoke
The hushed and tired voices
The anticipation of motion
This is the right place
The rain and the night air

The autobahn waiting
En route-in motion
I am real and filled with purpose
Not like when I am sitting in my room
In the other world
What a great night this is

9.4.90 Munich Germany: In a restaurant eating alone on a night off. All around me, talk and laughter over the music. Body is in pain, too much road in the last 9 months. The time passes so quickly. I stare at my calendar. Third trip to Europe this year.

The road keeps me alive. If it wasn't for the constant motion and work I would have blown out years ago. It's the only way to get rid of the pain that follows me. I'm not an artist. I am a reaction to life. I know that I'm not as strong as life, perhaps that's why I drag it kicking and screaming down the road. It's my life but it's not. I can control it to a certain extent. The parts I can't control rip me up and keep me moving. I want to get old on the road, disappear without a trace. Take years to learn and unlearn, to learn to forget. Impossible for me now, a challenge for later on. You can go as far as you want on this motherfucker.

9.11.90 Bordeaux France: Night off, hotel room # I've lost count. The bed takes up most of the room, hard to walk around. Smash my eyes out, fuck it. 8 hour drive, maybe they'll fall out on their own. This endless trail of lit up boxes. The boxed life. Bonnie and Clyde overdubbed in French on the television. If I could remember what your face looked like I could better imagine what it would be like to touch you. Hours ago I saw you in my mind. It was just a flash, couldn't hold onto it. Days go by without name. Tuesday could be Friday, dayless, dateless. Coltrane playing on my tape machine. Coming up on midnight. Your eyes, I have been trying to remember what they looked like when I stared into them. Exhaustion turns everything into an endless expanse of road. I'll take it though. Short tour, long tour, whatever. I was thinking the other day when we were at some gas station, how great it will be to tour this coming winter. Touring by myself in the cold, it's a great test. The guys in the band don't like it because they say that it makes their hands cold. It's ok though, I like touring on my own better anyway. But the bottom line is I'll take a tour anytime, anywhere, hot or cold. Canada, hell even Italy. Even England, and that's saying a lot seeing how crummy it is there. Anywhere is better than my room for more than 5 days straight. I wonder if you like me, what you think of me, what you think of everything. I wonder what your hair smells like, how it would feel on my chest. I should have smashed that piece of shit in Pisa the other night. Taken that bottle he threw at my head and shoved it down his throat. Someone told me how they saw Michael Stipe catch a bottle in the face in Vienna Austria in the same club that I played with the Flag in '83. Things are different there now. It was enjoyable smacking those 3 guys, not to mention cutting that guy's head open with the glass a while ago in good old Vienna town.

Chris and I walked to a post office today during a rest stop. We asked for stamps for mail to America. The man laughed at us. If you saw the river and the bridges and buildings, centuries old, you might think that a postcard to a country of hotheaded murderers is a joke. I might be able to convince you to get together with me. But even if you wanted to, it would be a bad idea. I don't work well up close. I am abusive and I don't know when it starts or where it comes from. Must keep moving. These hotel rooms are good. No one knows where I am. I would never want to hurt you but I know that I would. I wouldn't know when to stop either, happens every time. Better off on the road. Happiness chokes me. There's nothing I could tell you that wouldn't turn you away. I can cough and spit out thousands of miles of black pavement. Miles of stinking men's rooms. A planet of stench. I don't want to alienate you. Years ago I would have been able to get around all this and get to you. But now, I'll take the long tour, the short tour, winter, summer, bus, train, plane. Motion is a disease. A beautiful plague. A fever that burns my dreams.

9.18.90 Frankfurt Germany: Waiting for the flight out. Outside on the street the drunks argue and laugh. The hauptbahnhof is a few blocks away. The junkie dead collect and drool. Tonight I was on the autobahn. Clear night, stars, pine trees. Motion is all. I am hooked. Those truckers, the hard faraway look in their eyes. I know this is where I belong.

10.5.90 ? Georgia: Big moon on the rivers we cross. Roads full of debris and sadness. Old music shifting on the radio. The smell of gasoline on my hands. The woman at the diner said that all the other employees were either in AA, NA or "drug fiends." How many times down this road? Station to station of Exhaustion. Keep moving fast enough, enough of the time without looking back. You won't see the pieces of yourself fall and shatter. Crackling voice on the phone re-enforces the distance. One ear to the receiver, so you're already only half listening to the voice talking to you from the other world. The world that isn't addicted to motion. Miles go by. Stare at the cracks in your hands. Smell the gasoline, fall into yourself further. Roy Orbison was on the FM tonight. "Oh Pretty Woman" doesn't do anything to me anymore. That was over with 50 thousand miles ago. The truckstop near the river with the beautiful Indian name. The man inside fixing CB radios and telling jokes for the truckers gathered around, watching him work at his folding table. Country music, stale lights, dry air. Later on the moving road, the desperate mortal artery. I watch the Road Men slam by. Sitting high up in their mad cubicles, shielded by glass and steel. Enshrouded by dead insects and bird blood. I see the tail end of a truck pull away "Over Nite" across its back. We're all going to die out here, in transit.

10.9.90 Tucson AZ: The man with the swastika tattooed on his chest helped us load our gear into the shitty club. "I'm glad you guys don't have much stuff, just as soon as I get your stuff in I can go home and get my dick sucked again...this place used to be a shit country-western bar, no one ever comes here." The Southwest is filled with sadness. The sun takes so long to set. Seemingly motionless it hangs, painting everything with deep resounding sorrow. It mourns the earth before finally dropping out of sight. Rolling along the 10 West. Every town looks like a ghost town. Like they built them so they could have a place to leave. So many dead ends. The heat paralyzes, holds everything in its grip. These shit kickers, they have eyes of stone that fix upon you with a vice grip. They stare right thru you like a hot moving desert night stares thru you. A fat man staggers thru the dressing room. "Yea, it's dead out there tonight, deader than hell. Almost as dead as when John Doe was here..." Drinking, smoking, broken knuckles, jail time, tattoos, missing teeth, motorcycles, poverty and violence. America's glittering hollow dream lying on its side. The oasis dried up a long time ago. So much sadness out here in this sand and cactus sprawl. In less than an hour we go onstage to shoot electricity thru this empty desert night.

10.29.90 ? New York: In a cold beer barn. When we came in, we saw this big barrier in front of the stage. We asked the man if he could remove it. The guy said no it keeps the people off the stage and that's good for the kids because the bouncers beat the shit out of them any chance they get and that's the way it is. The barn is out on a small highway in the middle of the sticks. Danzig played here last night and they only drew a few hundred people. This place reminds me of the places I played when I was in Black Flag. Cold rooms in the middle of nowhere, staffed by nasty coked out jaded burners. This whole place is cold. The toilets don't work. The walls are covered with moronic displays of sexual frustration. This is the kind of place that would make you miss your girlfriend if you had one. Makes you think of your room at home and makes you want to be there right now. 3 or 4 nights in a row in a place like this and part of you dies. Like you could ever hope to translate the boredom and depression that a place like this generates. The attraction I have for these places I will never understand. Perhaps it's because it's so far away from their world that I feel like I can breathe. In a place like this I know what the deal is. I know my place, there is purpose and pain. Without movement, pressure and confrontation, life is an embarrassment.

10.30.90 Somewhere: The road wins. The road always wins. There before you. Longer, straighter and harder than you'll ever be. You can't aspire to genius like that. Go ahead, challenge the road and lose it all. Once you have allowed its black blood to mix with your own, you are owned. When you try to leave you are pulled back in. That is until you are chewed up and spat out, broken and dreamless. The road wants all of you. I was close to a woman once. I tried to get away from the road to see her. The road put a hex on me. Confused my words and made me see thru her. She called me names and told me that she didn't want someone that was never there. Woman after woman removed by the road. So I ride alone. Even amongst them I am alone. The road knows the end of the story before you sing the first verse. Winter is coming again. The road will be cold and impossible. I will be there.

5.14.91 Dayton OH: Selby and Don Bajema just got back from a spoken tour of Europe. From talking to Don it sounded like a piece of shit. I've got to hand it to Don though. No matter what, he will always give someone the benefit of the doubt. The whole thing was booked thru Dietmar and man did he fuck it up. There were no flyers up, no one knew that they were in town. Don's name was never on any of the listings. No train reservations, nothing. They didn't even have money to eat at some points. Sounds like the only thing that went smoothly was the plane flights that I booked for them a few weeks ago. Don said that Dietmar looked like he had a lot on his mind. This is no excuse. Here's the fucking deal: The road has a code. You don't break the code. You don't fuck with your men on the road. Dietmar broke all codes. How the fuck can you let down Selby? Fucking with Don isn't good either. Don can take anything, that guy can sleep on nails and be fine. But Selby? On that alone, Dietmar has lost his credibility with me. I like him as a person because I know he's a good guy, but after this upcoming tour never again. That's just the way it is. You don't break code twice. Not with me you don't. I feel like shit after hearing that I put these guys on the road with this bullshit. I didn't know, I figure when Dietmar says it's happening, it is. Now I know different. I've been on some bad ones. They last forever.

6.18.91 8:28 PM Los Angeles CA: Motion sickness. I've got it bad. Been home for a few days and I never want to see another one of them again. They call on the phone and it's torture. The only thing that makes sense is to get back out there where anything can happen. The tour of Europe was good. I'm ok when I'm out there. When I'm here, the voices get me. I can't take them. Some guy called me today, how the hell he got my number I'll never know. What the fuck is my problem? I had to do two interviews the other day. It was like getting teeth pulled. It was never this bad before. The phone has become an enemy. I am complaining like a fucking child but fuck it, it's the way I feel right now.

The night is here and I'm playing Sonny Rollins and Coltrane. It's getting better by degrees. Slowly the pieces are settling and I'm not wishing I was going 150 Km an hour down the autobahn. Motion sickness gets you coming and going. Makes all the words come out strange and fucked up. Makes me unable to deal with the reality of these people that don't travel 600 Km a day. If you don't do it then you don't know how to deal with someone that does and vice versa.

Let's not talk when we meet, we can nod and move on. There's no need for words, smiles or questions. Life is in passing anyway. All in passing.

MONSTER

Depression has settled deep inside me. For weeks now I cannot write. I cannot relate to people. I don't talk to them unless I am pressed to do so. I usually become abusive. I am violent by nature and at times it becomes hard to control myself. It is at its worst when I am depressed. Depression is with me. I am depression. My soul. A steel plate in my head. A trap door. A drain. Yes, it's like I am being drained by a huge leech. Rotten parasite, constant companion along for the ride dragging myself thru myself. How long will this one last, when will it release me from its grip. I don't know. I am convinced that it has nothing to do with me. I avoid people when I'm like this, they always make me feel worse. They look at me and ask what the problem is. My first impulse is to hit the person. I feel my throat tighten. I choke myself, punishment for being alive.

There's a dark cloud that hangs over me. I can't get to it. I am not feeling sorry for myself. I know that there are people that go thru this all their lives. I am a product of depression. It is the driving force in my life. I am not creative or smart. I think about killing myself all the time, like a lot of people. Sometimes it makes so much sense that it's all I can do to hang in there until the cloud passes. At the time it makes pure logical sense. That's when I rebel against myself and hang on. I torture myself with life. I exercise my body merely to taunt it, to cause it pain and make it hurt. To make it scream.

Basement. Dungeon. A long walk alone. Alone everywhere. Alone when I am with them. The stage is a perfect place for me. It is the truest place I know. It causes me pain like I have never experienced anywhere else. It is perverse and disgusting. All things brought to a boil. All is shown, all is known. I'm turned inside out for all to see. A freak with all the lights on. Sickness, desperate sickness. Isolation so heavy that I hate myself into sleep afterwards. They come up to me with their words of praise. It never makes sense to me why anyone would like to see something like that. I'm told that they know what I mean and that they feel the same way sometimes. I feel sorry for them. You can't know what someone else is feeling. As soon as you let that lie go, the real world opens its ugly jaws and swallows you whole.

Long ago I threw out the idea that the world was against me, trying to undermine all that I was trying to do. I used to think the same thing about life itself. I used to think that life was hunting me down and trying to destroy me. I have found that to be a big load of shit. It's always the easiest way out, to blame your problems on someone else, something else. I threw out the ideas that the world and life were my enemies. I found that I was protecting myself from the real enemy that I had not yet dealt with, myself. As soon as that was stripped away I saw things more clearly. I also stopped talking to people and became more withdrawn than usual.

I am a monster. I don't understand. Too many things cause me pain. I want to get lost. I want to escape my mind. I don't want to battle my mind again. The last time was too heavy and I lost. I want to walk until I disappear into nothing. Where is nowhere? How do I get there? Can I find it in the night? If it's anywhere, it's in the night, somewhere in the night. That feeling, like you're wearing a cloak of darkness. A secret wrapped in a secret, self protected. It's good to get a break from yourself.

I fell into my room. Got away from the streets and the noise. I'm looking at the walls, they look good to me right now. Slowly I forget them and their mind polluting words. I don't know how to handle praise. I feel like a con man when I stand there and take it from them. I feel like a commercial. I do it all wrong. I don't know what right is but I know that I am doing it all wrong.

I love dreamless sleep. Dreams tell me too much, sometimes

the less I know the better. Let me explain. The more I look, the more I see. Like the time I had my arms around her. I looked at her, I looked in. I tried to stop my eyes. I wanted to stop seeing. It happened like it always happens. I saw thru her. I look into myself. I don't stop when I should stop. I dissect myself. I see thru myself, I expose myself to myself. I don't like what I see. The less I see the better. Do you look too deeply, do you see too much? I have a bad ability, it's like a curse. I can make anything look bad to me by looking at it too long. I always look too long. I see thru love and affection. I see desperation in praise. I see hate and jealousy. I see it in myself. I want to walk in the desert tonight. I want the wind to pass over me. I want to let the poison bleed thru the soles of my feet into the desert floor. I want to starve the monster. I want to punish it with thoughts of clean night wind. The monster will kick and bellow, it can't take a direct shot. It cannot take the pain of painlessness.

The iron door slams shut. A convict stares the paint off a wall. There is no next time. There is only a flickering recollection of last time. History is vacant and meaningless. Thoughts of the past bring pain that cannot be measured. Thoughts of tomorrow are nightmares wrapped in reality. He can no longer prove his past. He can no longer prove himself. He throws the shackles away and lands hard in the present. He closes his eyes and opens them again. The wall is still there. He falls deep inside himself. Relentless until it kills you all the way.

When you're finally a world away. When you have left them, when the pain and confusion has fallen away. What then? What do you do with the vacancy? What do you do with all the time that you spent hating, wanting what they had. Wanting to feel like them. What do you with the hours, with the thoughts. What do you do with the freedom. You learn that you spent a lot of time thinking about them. You were a part of them more than you had ever suspected. You disgust yourself, you weren't above it after all. You were with them all the time. Speaking the language that you proudly thought you didn't know a word of. Vacancy's vacuum. I feel a duty to fill all the cracks, to shove light into all the dark corners.

The pain eases away, your step gets lighter. You're so used to the tension that now life is new and strange again. You let them and the world they rode in on leave, and it's a new world. Your new world. Welcome to your new world, your new room, your new reality. You trip and fall a lot, it's good to fall.

I don't blame people for the way they make me feel. I used to, it's good to let them go. I used to cause myself so much pain at their feet. They didn't know what the hell was going on. There I was bleeding at their doorstep, pointing my finger at them. Calling them heartbreakers, the dispatchers of despair. It was me all along.

What I know: I can't relate to them. When I try, I am filled with confusion and pain. I don't know what to do with words. When I talk, words take on other meanings. I don't get it right. I let go. Hard at first, missed the things that made me sick. To have a broken heart, to lose sleep over someone, to feel jealousy. Amazed at the depths and the lengths that they will go and the places they will take you if you attach to them. Years of my life living for them. Hoping to be lucky enough to be part of the human experience, their world. To dream their nightmares, to be on the team. To spend eternities, lifetimes, deaths. Rejecting them over and over yet running back happy to be given another chance to reject them again.

What a bad bucket of blood. To feel pain and feel good because you know that it's all yours and finding out that it's not. You got it from them. You're merely a tenant living off their scraps.

My pain defines me. Their pain, when ingested, distorts me. It weakens me, blinds me. I learn nothing, I don't grow. I run headlong into their jail. That's over with.

"Look it's a monster, he's walking alone. Look, he's pulling something out of his pocket. He threw it on the ground. Let's go see what it is. It's a black box, you open it...ok...look. It's sorrow misery and pain. It's loneliness and longing. Boy, he'll be sorry he lost these."

I've tried some stupid things in my time. Gone to extremes to try and get away from things in my head that I knew were trying to kill me. Hard to swallow when you see yourself as the enemy. Only you could put yourself thru this shit. I have tried to ignore myself, failing miserably every time.

Have you ever fallen in on yourself? Like you're the coal mine and the miner? Happens to me all the time. I sit alone after a show. The smell of their cigarette smoke in my hair and a ringing roar in my ears. I look at the floor and I think about them. I have nothing of myself to grab onto. I know better than to hold onto them. I know the mindless stupid pain that attachment brings. Life is hard enough. I remember their faces telling me what to do. All that heat. Another night, another freak-out. Another life thrown into the abyss. I look inside, nothing. I wish for a signal to tell me that I am still alive. I wonder why I don't turn into a pile of salt and fall into the cracks in the floor. I wonder if any of me comes out with all that sweat, like maybe I sweat my brain out up there. I close my eyes and listen. I hear pieces of myself falling and breaking at the bottom. I'm hollow, a shell, a name for someone to call. I hear the black wings of Loneliness beating overhead. I see Despair coming over, waving and smiling. I send Despair packing. I shoot Loneliness down and stomp on its frail body. I come back to myself. It takes longer as the years go by. These people don't realize what they're seeing. they think that they are getting entertained. If they knew how real all this was they would be turned off.

Beware the drains. Here they come. Smiling, hands outstretched. They want to test your stamina. They will see what you got, how you'll stand up to the test. Beware the leeches. The eyes, they look like they could move in for awhile. They look friendly, like you could get close. Beware the trap, don't allow your perception to destroy you. The best intent can tear you to shreds and leave you bloodless, thoughtless, nowhere. You want to attach, to leech someone for awhile. For a night, for a few lifeless hours. Someone to listen to, doesn't matter what they're saying as long as they're saying it to you. You need to put the bite on someone and hold them for as long as it takes for you to get what you need. Call it whatever you want. Maybe it's ugly, well ok. The world is an ugly place. It doesn't understand anyone's anything, never did. Where are the leeches tonight. Maybe in the mirror.

Walking wounded and dazed. Is there anyone alive out there tonight? I hear rain falling, I hear cars passing, I see shapes moving but I can't be sure. I have a rotten re-occurring feeling that rips thru me. A desperate longing for what I don't know. I walk, thinking that it might come to me, that I might be able to get my hands around its throat and strangle it. I want to kill it because it wants to kill me. I say kill all the fucking enemies in my brain. The monster stalks the streets in search of itself. Regret, fuck that guy. Despair, shoot him. Loneliness, come forward. I want to disfigure you. I want to turn you on yourself and make you see what you do to people. I want you to see the blood and the anger. I want you to feel the sullen lump that finds itself in my throat when you come in. I want to lock you up in solitary and watch you destroy yourself. I'm going to make sure you go as slow as possible. I want you to taste every drop. You're going to find out what hell is like. You're going to see that it's you. To make things as bad as I can, I'm going to give you little breaks from yourself. I'll give you shot glasses full of the finest companionship. I'll get you hooked. Then when all you want is that next shot I'm going to cut you off and you'll be left all alone with yourself.

And then you will know what we all know. You will scream like we all scream. You will feel the pain. I don't know if you'll be able to survive yourself. That's a terrifying thought isn't it. Well good, we all go thru it. Now it's your turn...Yea well I can't find any of those fuckers tonight. I keep walking. I walk the dark streets, the dark thoughts, the dark minds, dark deaths. I look for a way to get rid of the poison. It seems like I can confront myself all day long but can't go on from there. Confrontation takes little thought. You just get up and go. I have always been good at the things that take little thought. Sure you can confront, but what you do next, that's what tells you what you are. The human experience can make you every stupid name in the book. I try to not let the human experience make an ass out of me more than three times a minute.

Have you ever tried to outrun yourself. Lose yourself in a crowd, hide from yourself in the stall of a bathroom. Take on a new attitude to fool yourself into thinking that you're someone else, me too. Same thing every time. At the end, it's always you holding onto yourself. Out of breath, self humiliated, hot footed, red handed and hopelessly human.

I find such emptiness in your television shopping mall eyes. If I had a heart to break, I swear you would break it. How far does one have to go before the pain falls away. I don't want to shoot myself in the head anymore. I'm tired of that money business. I'm tired of my brain. I want to remove parts, burn parts out. Do you get tired of the language that they speak, the things that they do? They shove dirt into my thoughts. Can't wait for the sun to go down today. I can come out at night, I can lose myself at night. Walk and forget, walk and unload. I can't make words work. If I could say the right thing to you, maybe you could tell me what it is that's killing me. I wouldn't mind it if you saved me. Some would hold it against you. Turn it on you. Try to take all your good and ram it into your guts so hard that the whole world turned black and all you could see was scar tissue. I think of you a lot. You and me walking along in the parking lot at night, our shoulders rubbing against each other as we listen to our hushed voices. We're both damaged and beautiful. We know the order of order and the order of disorder. We have both been hunted and nearly destroyed by weaklings with big ideas. We know the night. I was always hoping that you would turn out to be strong. Stronger than I had ever had thought possible. You would be able to save me. You would be able to stop time for a second. You would make a miracle happen and show me. You would take the pain away. You would fold me up, put me in your pocket and use me later.

Hack chew and spit. You've got to get them out of your life. They will haunt you until the end of your days. They'll make you want to die, it's a bad price to pay. If I could have a bullet for every time my mother and father made me want to die, I would have enough to slaughter every pig that needed it. I don't want to be one. It's not my contempt for humanity that keeps me from being a father. It's the word. I'm a lot of bad things, you hear what the little shitheads say...but a father, I never want to be a father. All I want do is fight and kill mine. I want to engage him in combat. I want him to make me fight for my life. I want to take his so I can live out what's left of mine. I deny myself life by not killing him. I think he wants me to, I can feel it in my fist-like thought. You have to get away from them. I hope they didn't hurt you. I hope they didn't fuck you up. I wish they had let your mind free years before you had to rip it from their grasp. Think about it. Survey the damage done. Don't do it all at once, you might stop traffic.

I wish you well on your trip. Life is boring and short. The process is hard. Leaves scars and then just leaves.

61 DREAMS 1986-1989

#1: I'm riding on a train. I see a bat clinging to the chair in front of me. I start to hit it. The first blows don't do anything. I keep hitting it. Finally the bat's eye fills up with blood but now the bat starts to grow.

#2: A pig has me pinned against a wall. He looks into my eyes. His eyes are blue. I'm scared but smiling. He starts to kiss me. I can taste his tongue. It tastes like coffee and tobacco.

#3: I am in the drugstore at Wisconsin and Calvert in Washington DC. I'm heading for the door as I know the bus is coming and I have to go across the street to get it. I'm almost out the door and Davo comes up and asks me how to get to Alban Towers apartments. He says that Gone has an instore to do up there and he needs me to make him a map. I make him a map even though it's just up the street. I give him the map and run out the door to see the bus going up the street past me. I run like hell and finally catch up to the bus. I'm about to get on when I realize that I have left my book bag back at the drugstore. I had put it down when I was giving instructions to Davo.

#4: Greg Ginn is sleeping. He opens his eyes and sees a large window in front of him. Across the window is a piece of white cloth with the Black Flag logo on it. A coffin comes smashing thru the window. Down on the street a group of kids run away laughing. They run to a hearse and tell the driver that it's time to make a getaway as they all pile into the back. The driver yawns and slowly gets in the hearse and drives it away.

#5: Ian is walking down the street with a bunch of kids behind him. He is wearing a plaid suit and talking to a reporter who is holding a microphone in front of his face.

#6: Ian is a contestant on a television game show. The MC spins the wheel, the crowd cheers. Ian holds up a blue poker chip. He looks at the guy and says "I can't have all that because of this?" and throws the poker chip over his shoulder.

#7: I'm on the shore of a lake. There's a series of rocks that stand above the water. On some of the larger rocks there's some alligators sunning themselves. Ian comes up to me and tells me that I should come over and see some gator eggs that he found. I look over and I see Katie standing next to me. The three of us walk over the rocks to where the gators are and one by one they all slide off into the water. I see two black eggs floating in the water. Ian is standing next to me, he looks down into the water and says "Eels." I look down and see a large eel coming out of the water with its mouth open.

#8: I am in a room with Greg. We are over looking a large concert arena. The bass player from W.A.S.P. comes in and tells us that his band is stronger than ever.

#9: I'm in a gymnasium. I came in with a group of people but I don't know who they are. All of a sudden men with guns are shooting at us. I try to remember how I came in so I can get out. I run thru a door and pass a man in a cook's uniform. I know that he wants to kill me.

#10: A woman straps me into a chair. I remember that there's a place that will inject music into your head so you'll have music continually for weeks without having to turn on a stereo. I assume that I'm in this place. She sticks a large needle into my head and I can feel juice go in.

#11: I am following some men down a street, they don't seem aware of my presence. I come up to them and ask if I could get a handgun from them. I tell them I want a .357 or a .44 with an eight inch barrel. One of them nods yes. I follow them into a candy store but lose them once inside.

#12: I'm in this room with a man and a woman. I get up and go over to the woman and start grabbing at her breasts. She tries to get away but I catch her and bite her into her back. The man comes over and grabs me, he says "Look what you've done." The woman is bleeding thru her shirt.

#13: I get handcuffed to a chin-up bar. The bar is high off the ground. If I don't hold the bar with my hands, my wrists will get mangled by the cuffs.

#14: I'm handcuffed to a chair. Someone is putting a joint in my mouth. I smoke it.

#15: I go to the dentist. From down the hall I hear a guitar playing, it's Greg. I go into the office and see him, he has short hair dyed black. We look at each other and say nothing. The dentist comes into the office and tells me it's time to go. I leave.

#16: I'm in a parking lot. I drop my pool ball, it rolls away. I look for it. The lot is covered with pool balls. The cement has turned to grass. I pick up hundreds of balls, none of them are mine. Right color, wrong number.

#17: I'm at the Inglewood Forum with Joe. We are watching Jimi Hendrix play. I go backstage to talk to him. I say "I'm looking forward the cd of the Winterland show, it should be great." He says "Yea, it's not the whole show, it's part of the show with some compilation cuts on the end." I nod and I'm about to ask him another question but he waves me off and goes onto the stage. The crowd goes wild. I return to my seat and tell Joe that I thought he was better last time.

#18: I try to fuck this girl. I get my cock part way in, it won't go any farther. I look down at my cock, it's covered with blood.

#19: Someone tells me that my mother is dead. All these people are crying about it, me too. I get taken to a room. There's a casket on the floor. Someone opens the lid, there's a body bag inside with the zipper half way down near the head. I don't look in.

#20: I'm in a ditch, I am digging with some other men. My mother comes up to me. She is happy and smiling. She wants me to pick out a coffin for her.

#21: I'm in a room with a girl. My father comes in, he looks drunk. He's holding a bottle half full of yellow liquid. He grabs one of the girl's breasts. She starts to cry. He leaves the room.

#22: I'm walking down the street. I see my father drive by. He's in a station wagon. He's driving into people and causing accidents. He's smiling.

#23: John Lennon's mother is selling John Lennon dolls. The doll's mouths are sewn shut like the mouths of shrunken heads.

#24: My father puts his dogs on me. I run away.

#25: I'm in a car wreck. My back is broken. I'm on all fours. I'm loaded into an ambulance. The attendant shoves a plastic bag into my mouth. I start to suffocate. I try to get it out. I can't do it.

#26: I shoot a man. He dies on my front lawn. All the neighbors come and look. Every once in a while I come out and shoot him again because he keeps getting up.

#27: A naked woman is walking on a lawn. A male voice asks "Where are you going?" She does a back bend and says "Over and under." All there is to see is the space between her legs, she has a large gaping anus and a pronounced vulva. The voice asks her if she likes some bank. She says "Why should I go to that bank when mine has Interteller?" At that moment she stands up and all this viscous liquid comes rushing from her vagina. She lies down and a man about one foot high with a large cock walks between her legs and starts fucking her. She smiles and lets out a long sigh.

#28: I'm in Vietnam. I crawl thru some bushes and come upon a clearing. I see a small plane moving slow. Behind the plane is a group of jets. I guess that an airstrike is about to happen. I pull back into the bushes. A small boy drops on top of me from overhead. We crawl back to camp. I keep telling the boy that it's very dangerous around here. He won't listen to me. At the camp a man starts talking to me. I tell him that I don't think I'll be coming home from this. He starts laughing and says "All that time in Hollywood California and even that can't get you home from this place." I start shoving him and he keeps laughing. I punch him but nothing happens.

#29: I go to a girl's house. There's a man sitting on the couch, he's grinning at me. The girl comes out of a room and motions for me to come in, I go. She gives me two presents. I ask her if she's giving me these because she wants to be rid of me. She says "Yes!"

#30: Ted Nugent is doing an interview telling about how he got shot in the face. He points to a hole in the side of nose and refers to god as "Big Daddy."

#31: I'm living at my mother's house. An old girlfriend is living there too. I don't know this until she comes out of a room. I look at her and ask her if she's living here and she says yes. She leaves and gets in my mother's car and drives away.

#32: I finish a show and I'm backstage catching my breath. All these people are coming up to me and telling me that they like what I do. I look over and see a girl that I used to hang out with, she is kissing a man. They break, look at me, and leave arm in arm.

#33: U2 is on stage. Edge starts a song and screws it up. The rest of the band yells at him and the crowd boos him loudly. He starts again with the exact same notes and the place goes wild and the rest of the band smiles and starts to play. Greg and I are watching and laughing as we imitate the lameness of his playing.

#34: I'm in the stairwell of a house that I used to live in with my mother. I'm lacing my shoe. When I'm done I'm going to kill myself. Inside the house there's a girl in a room waiting for me to do it. Music is playing, the same song as when the kids are filing past the coffin in the movie River's Edge.

#35: I go to a record store. Dennis Hopper is there. I go up to him and tell him that I'm a big fan of his. He tells me to fuck off.

#36: The sun is setting on a grassy field. In the middle of the field there are three coffins. As I approach the coffins I ask the man next to me who they are. He tells me that the one in the middle is his father. I look at the man walking with me, it's Joe Carducci.

Soon they bury his dad and I watch Joe cry. I am also consumed with grief.

#37: I'm going to kill this woman, my friends are going to kill her baby. They can't do it. I look down at the baby who is in a pile of leaves. The baby is bleeding out of its head. I look away. When I look back I see that the baby's head has come off. I bury the body in the leaves. I turn around. The police are there and they start questioning me.

#38: I have a machine gun and I'm shooting people as they walk by my house. It's night time but I can see them. One guy comes thru the door and I unload an entire clip into him but he keeps coming at me. Flesh is falling off his face, his skull is made of metal. He smiles and falls. I hear a voice. I turn and shoot. It's Bernie Wandel. The bullet blows part of his head off. I tell him that he's going to die and that I'm sorry. He says it's ok.

#39: I'm in a bookstore with a girl, we're listening to a man talk about politics. I think he sucks. He looks into the crowd and says that he can't find a good breakfast anywhere. The girl I'm with gets up and says "Do you like your breakfast with espresso?" She takes his hand and they leave.

#40: There is a blue beetle crawling by my foot. I crush it. The beetle turns into a headless chicken and shit starts to come from its headless stump.

#41: A girl I went out with a long time ago is lying on a table with her shirt off and I am kissing her stomach. Another girl I was having sex with moments before comes into the room. The girl on the table says to the other girl "I am Henry's girl."

#42: I walk up to this girl that I used to go out with and ask her if she likes me. She just stares and says nothing.

#43: I crush a man's skull with a rock. I run and hide and come out every once in awhile to ask people if the police are looking for me.

#44: I'm in bed with a girl. A naked girl walks into the room. I try to fuck both of them. They leave the room laughing.

#45: I'm in a car and I'm driving the wrong way on the road. People are beeping at me and swerving to avoid me.

#46: A spider and a fish try to fuck. It doesn't work.

#47: I have to fuck a guy in a movie.

#48: I'm in the studio doing vocals for the In My Head album. I have never heard the songs before. All the lyrics are by Greg and they're about how much he hates me.

#49: I'm in bed with a girl. One by one people start to file into the room. I don't mind that, the only thing I'm worried about is that one of them might be a girl that I hang out with. One of the girls is one that I'm very close to. I can see the hurt on her face. I see another girl too, she's laughing. I try to sneak out of the room.

#50: Two girls and a man hold a baby in front of a mirror. They strangle it.

#51: Two girls and a guy have sex in a crib.

#52: I'm in a room with Robert Duvall, he tells me that everything I say is bullshit.

#53: John Coltrane has invented a new kind of music that will save the world.

#55: I'm on a plane, we are making a long left. The plane levels out and is a few hundred feet away from the side of a mountain.

#55: I have just finished a talking gig. I can barely talk. I'm mad at myself because of how bad my voice has become.

#56: I'm strapped to a chair. Three people surround me, taking turns sticking needles into my arm. Every time one of them is about to stick one in, one of them yells "Needle!" The last time, they all yell it at once and plunge needles into my hand.

#57: David Bowie, my mother, G. Gordon Liddy and I get out of a van to go into shopping mall. I'm asking Bowie a lot of questions about his music. He doesn't want to talk to me. Liddy goes into the mall to complain. My mother says that she remembers him from the Nixon era and it's no use in trying to stop him. The rest of us decide to go in and get some food while he is complaining. I am wearing a blue sweatshirt, half on and half off. Bowie asks me why I have my shirt like that. I tell him that it's part of the way the gang I'm in dresses. At that moment, a man comes from behind a pile of boxes and starts shooting at me.

#58: I am a father. My son runs up to a boy his age and punches him in the face. I apologize to the boy's mother.

#59: Joe and I are standing on the street. I take out a pistol and shoot a passerby in the head. I make comment to Joe that the gun isn't very loud.

#60: A man comes up to me and tells me that I can buy a virgin girl for fifty dollars and she will be delivered to me after the show. I give him the money. After the show, she's backstage. I tell her that I think this fifty dollar virgin business is the stupidest thing I've ever heard of. She leaves.

#61: The band is playing but I can't find them. I'm in a hallway singing without a mike. There's a boy standing in front of me. The only words that come out of my mouth are the lyrics to Cure songs. The boy is into it. I start acting like Robert Smith.

I KNOW YOU

I know you
You were too short
You had bad skin
You couldn't talk to them very well
Words didn't seem to work
They lied when they came out of your mouth
You tried so hard to understand the others
You wanted to be part of what was happening
You saw them having fun
Seemed like such a mystery
Almost magic
You thought that there was something wrong with you
You would look in the mirror trying to find the flaw
You thought that you were ugly
And that everybody was looking at you
So you learned to be invisible
To look down
To avoid conversation
The hours, days, weekends
The weekend nights
Alone
Where were you,
The basement, the attic, your room?
Working some job?
Just to have something to do?
Just to have a place to put yourself?
Just to have a way to get away from them
Staying away from the ones
That made you feel so strange
And ill at ease inside yourself

Did you ever get invited to one of their parties
You sat and wondered if you would go or not
For hours you imagined what might transpire
If they would laugh at you
If you would know what to do
If you would have the right things on
If they would notice that you came from a different planet
Did you get all brave in your thoughts
Like you were going to be able to go in there
Deal with it and have a great time?
Did you think that you might be the "life of the party?"
That all these people were going to talk to you
And you would find out that you were wrong
And that you had a lot of friends
And you weren't so strange after all?
Did you end up going?
Did they mess with you?
Did they single you out?
Did you find out that you got invited
Because they thought you were so weird?
I think I know you
You spent a lot of time full of hate
A hate that was as pure as sunshine
A hate that saw for miles
A hate that kept you up at night
A hate the filled your every waking moment
A hate that carried you for a long time
Yes, I think I know you
You couldn't figure out what they saw in the way they lived
Home was not home
Your room was home
A corner was home
Anywhere they weren't

That was home
I know you
You're sensitive
You hide it
You fear getting stepped on one more time
It seems that when you show a part of yourself
That is the least bit vulnerable
Someone takes advantage of you
One of them steps on you
They mistake kindness for weakness
But you know the difference
You've been the brunt of their weakness for years
Strength is something you know a bit about
You had to be strong to keep yourself alive
You know yourself very well now
You don't trust people
You know them too well
You try to find a special person
Someone you can be with
Someone you can touch
Someone you can talk to
Someone you won't feel so strange around
You found that they don't really exist
You feel closer to people on movie screens
Yea, I think I know you
You spend a lot of time daydreaming
People have made comment to that effect
Telling you that you're self involved and self centered
But they don't know, do they
About the long night shifts alone
About the years of keeping yourself company
All the nights you wrapped your arms around yourself
So you could imagine someone holding you

The hours of indecision
Self doubt
The intense depression
The blinding hate
The rage that made you stagger
The devastation of rejection
Well, maybe they do know
But if they do
They sure do a good job of hiding it
It astounds you how they can be so smooth
How they seem to pass thru life
As if life itself was some divine gift
It infuriates you to watch yourself
With your apparent skill in finding every way possible
To screw it up
For you life is a long trip
Terrifying and wonderful
Birds sing to you at night
The rain and the sun
The changing seasons are true friends
Solitude is a hard won ally
Faithful and patient
Yes I think I know you